JILL NORMAN
THE
CLASSIC
HERB
COOKBOOK

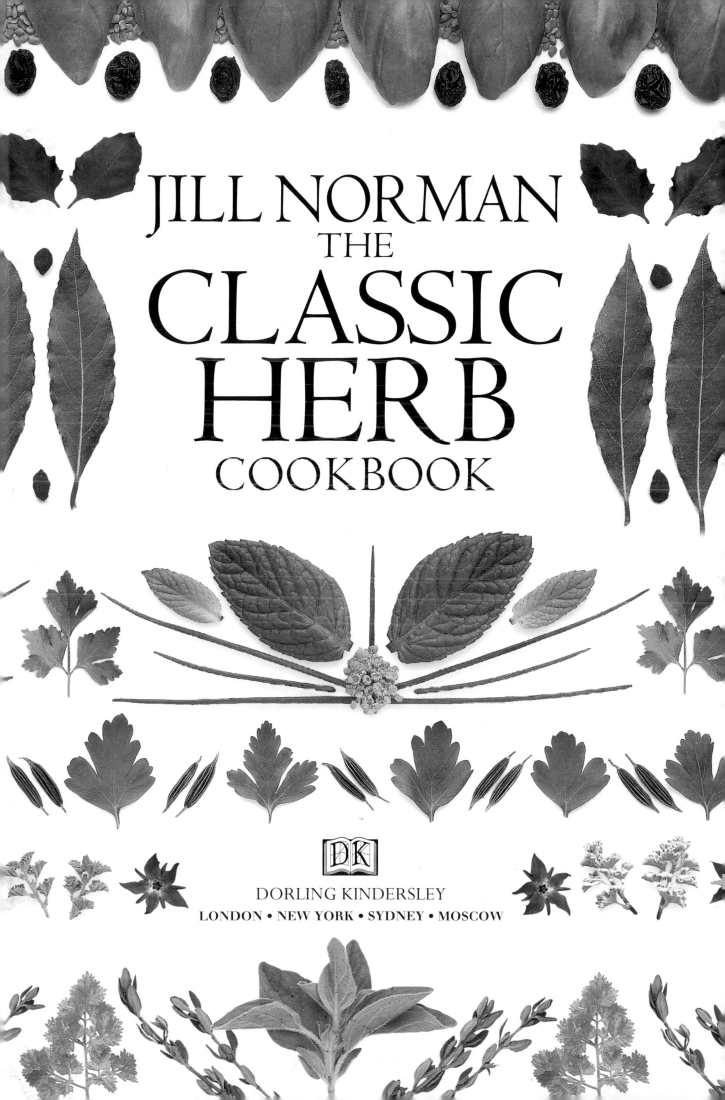

JILL NORMAN
THE
CLASSIC
HERB
COOKBOOK

DORLING KINDERSLEY
LONDON • NEW YORK • SYDNEY • MOSCOW

A DORLING KINDERSLEY BOOK

Project Editor
Pamela Brown

Art Editor
Julia Worth

Editorial Assistant
Lorraine Turner

Senior Art Editor
Tracey Clarke

Managing Editor
Fay Franklin

Managing Art Editor
Virginia Walter

Deputy Art Director
Carole Ash

Photography
Ian O'Leary

Home Economists
Nicola Fowler, Oona van den Berg, Sunil Vijayakar

Production Controller
Manjit Sihra

For Sasha and Mark

First published in Great Britain in 1997
by Dorling Kindersley Limited,
9 Henrietta Street, London WC2E 8PS
Reprinted in 1997

© 1997 Dorling Kindersley Limited, London
Text copyright © 1997 Jill Norman
Visit us on the World Wide Web at http://www.dk.com

A CIP catalogue for this book is available from
the British Library

ISBN 0 7513 0323 2

Reproduced in Italy by Scanner Services SRL
Printed and bound in Italy by A. Mondadori, Verona

CONTENTS
INTRODUCTION 6

A CATALOGUE OF HERBS 8

*A photographic guide detailing each
herb's traditional and current role, and how
best to prepare and use it.*

INTRODUCTION

*"Les fines herbes sont le parfum de la cuisine,
mais il faut en user avec la même discretion que
les parfums, afin de laisser à chaque mets son
goût particulier ou son individualité."*
CELESTINE EUSTIS, LA CUISINE CREOLE, 1903

The herb gardens of the past were orderly collections of plants for the kitchen and still room, for medicines, sweet waters, cosmetics and strewing herbs. Pot, salad and aromatic herbs were cultivated in profusion, and more plants were picked from the wild.

The distinction between herbs and leaf vegetables was seldom made whether for cooking or for salads. Herb soups, boiled puddings and pies contained spinach, leeks, beet tops, lettuce and chard as well as what we call herbs. At the end of the 17th century John Evelyn's *Acetaria* listed some 70 plants for use in salads – "a particular combination of certain crude and fresh Herbs", which could be dressed with oil, salt and vinegar.

Over time, some flavours that naturally complement each other have become "classics" in different cultures: sage with veal in Italy, tarragon with chicken in France, mint with lamb in Britain, coriander and chillies in Mexico, basil with tomatoes everywhere. Sometimes such traditional uses can appear arbitrary and inhibit experiment but, with the cross-fertilization of cuisines, adventurous variations occur more readily – witness the many "pesto" varieties based on coriander, dill, rocket and so on.

This book is an exploration of the way herbs are used in different cuisines. It offers suggestions for bringing new varieties or new uses for familiar herbs into the western repertoire. In writing it I made some discoveries, most of them rewarding, added greatly to my herb garden, and broadened my ideas about combinations of flavours. There remains ample scope for further exploration.

For most dishes fresh herbs are best. Supermarkets now carry a wide range, albeit at high prices. Middle Eastern or oriental shops (and a few enterprising greengrocers) have big bunches for the same price as the few supermarket sprigs. These are good places to look for new and unusual herbs, as are specialist nurseries. Most herbs are easy to grow in the garden or in pots.

Many herbs freeze successfully for a few months: they may look wilted but will retain their flavour. The French now market small packs of frozen leaves which are worth looking out for, as are the strong-flavoured herbs like oregano and tarragon preserved in oil. The herbs that dry well are those that retain their essential oil, and if they have been grown in a warm climate their aroma and flavour will be incomparably stronger. I was particularly pleased to come across Iranian dried herbs: their aroma is very fresh and pure.

Some herbs develop their flavours with long cooking – bay, oregano, rosemary, sage, tarragon, thyme; others are best added at the end of cooking – basil, chervil, chives, coriander, lemon balm and parsley.

There are classic herb mixtures but, essentially, combining herbs and other flavourings and the amounts to use are matters of personal taste. This is not an exact science: a teaspoon of chopped herbs will do little except garnish a dish of beans, although heavy-handedness is another extreme to avoid. Be judicious, always balancing the strong flavours with the mild, and use the combinations suggested here as a basis for trying out your own ideas.

A CATALOGUE OF HERBS

The following pages illustrate the wide range of herbs available to the cook, starting with the most popular. Where possible, different varieties are shown with notes on their properties and possible uses. On later pages, related plants — or those with similar flavours and aromas — are grouped together. Botanical names are given throughout to aid recognition.

BASIL

Ocimum basilicum

NATIVE TO INDIA, where it is sacred to Vishnu, basil reached the Mediterranean in ancient times. Still today, the air in many a Greek village is filled with a spicy aroma from pots of bush basil, although it is little used in the cooking. A tender plant, basil was raised from seed in northerly herb gardens for some 200 years, but its popularity had declined by the beginning of this century. Its recent revival is largely due to the increased interest in Provençal, Italian and, latterly, Thai cooking.

ANISE BASIL
O.b. 'Anise'
Has a clear anise flavour with a hint of bitterness. Used in south-east Asian cooking.

THAI BASIL
O.b. 'Horapha'
Clean peppery smell with hints of anise. Similar to anise basil but has narrower leaves.

PESTO SAUCE
The leaves of sweet basil are pounded with pine nuts to form the base of classic pesto sauce.

PURPLE or OPAL BASIL
O.b. var. purpurascens
A handsome plant with pink flowers; it will add colour to cream sauces or green salads.

LEMON BASIL
O.b. var. citriodorum
Light green leaves have a clean lemon fragrance; good with fish and in mixed salads.

CINNAMON BASIL
O.b. 'Cinnamon'
Pink flowers and a sweet, intense scent. Stir into bean and pulse dishes.

LETTUCE LEAF BASIL
O.b. var. crispum
The floppy leaves can be used to wrap foods for cooking. Similar flavour to sweet basil.

PURPLE RUFFLES BASIL
O.b. 'Purple Ruffles'
The frilled leaves grow quite large and are good in salads. Use them as sweet basil. There is also a green version.

CAMPHOR BASIL
O. kilimandscharicum

Strong camphor aroma; best in herb mixtures. If hard to find, add star anise to sweet basil.

AFRICAN BLUE BASIL
O. 'African Blue'

Handsome plant with mottled purple-green leaves smelling of pepper and liquorice. Use with rice, vegetables and stews.

GREEK BASIL
O.b. var. minimum

Neat bush with small leaves and a pungent peppery aroma. Good with rice and grains.

HOLY BASIL (TULSI)
O. sanctum

Used in Thai cooking. Has notes of clove and mint and a slight bitterness. If unavailable, add a little mint to sweet basil.

SWEET BASIL
O. basilicum

The most common and popular basil; the bright green aromatic leaves can be used for all western cooking.

AROMA & TASTE

Basil has an unmistakable spicy aroma followed by a warm flavour of clove and pepper, with notes of mint and liquorice.

CULINARY USES

Best known as the base of pesto sauce of Genoa and the related pistou of southern France, basil combines well with garlic, olive oil, lemon and tomatoes, both raw and cooked. Pepper and aubergine dishes benefit from basil, as do potatoes, beans and rice.

To retain aroma and flavour, it is best to use only a little during cooking and to add the rest at the end. Tearing rather than chopping the leaves also brings out the flavour better.

Sprigs of the edible flowers make an aromatic garnish or addition to a salad.

Thai cooks use three types of basil: *bai horabha* (Thai basil), the most similar to sweet basil, used in curry pastes and added to curries made with coconut milk; *bai gaprow* (holy basil), for curries without coconut milk, stir-fries, fish and chicken dishes; and *bai manglug* (sweet balsam basil, *O. canum*), added at the end of cooking for a lemon flavour.

Basil bruises easily so handle it carefully. It is best used fresh but can be frozen; dried or freeze-dried has little flavour. You can also preserve leaves, with a little salt between layers, in a jar of oil: they will turn black, but the flavour remains for some months. A purée, made with olive oil, can be kept in the refrigerator or frozen.

For key recipes, see pages 50, 60, 90, 94, 102, 108, 138.

MINT

Mentha species

PERENNIAL PLANTS, mostly native to central Asia and the Mediterranean basin, mints hybridize easily so there are many subspecies – and some confusion in their naming. A versatile flavouring, mint used sparingly provides a good backdrop for other herbs such as basil, dill and parsley. In oriental cooking it blends well with spices, notably ginger, cumin, cardamom and cloves.

PENNYROYAL
M. pulegium (upright form)
This has an intense, almost disagreeable, flavour. Formerly esteemed for stuffings and savoury puddings, it must be used with caution.

PINEAPPLE MINT
M. suaveolens 'Variegata'
Its pleasant fruity flavour is suited to summer punches and fruit salads, and to flavouring ricotta or cream cheese.

APPLE MINT
M. suaveolens
Has a light flavour of apple.

BLACK PEPPERMINT
M. × piperita var. piperita
A strong, fiery flavour. Its essential oil, which contains menthol, is used for liqueurs, confectionery and toothpaste.

LEMON MINT
M. piperita citrata 'Lemon'
A refreshing lemon note when you smell it. Use in salads, to make mint butter (good with grilled fish), and for drinks.

GINGER MINT
M. × gracilis 'Variegata'
Pungent and spicy: try it with black olives, feta cheese and good bread.

**EAU DE COLOGNE
MINT**
M. × piperita citrata
*The delicate flavour goes well
with vanilla to make little pots
de crème. Also called lemon,
orange and bergamot mint.*

BOWLES' MINT
M. × villosa alopecuroides
*Wilts rapidly, but is well worth
growing for its fine flavour.*

MOROCCAN SPEARMINT
M. spicata **'Moroccan'**
*Prized for its fine aroma and
taste, it is used in Morocco to
flavour sweet green tea.*

CURLED SPEARMINT
M. spicata **'Crispa'**
*Spearmint's many forms differ
in colour and flavour intensity.
Its light fragrance is perfect for
chilled pea and mint soup.*

TASHKENT SPEARMINT
M. spicata **'Tashkent'**
*Has a concentrated aroma and
flavour. An excellent choice for
making fresh chutney with
chillies and green mango.*

AROMA & TASTE
All the mints are highly
aromatic; the strong,
sweetish yet fresh smell is
instantly recognizable. The
taste is pleasantly warm
and pungent with a cooling
aftertaste.

CULINARY USES
In western cooking mint is
generally used fresh. It
enhances carrots, potatoes,
aubergines and all the
legumes. Its sharp yet sweet
character complements
grilled fish and roast or
grilled lamb, whether in a
marinade, as mint butter,
mint sauce or in a salsa.
Add it to tomato soup with
some chilli for a Latin
American flavour.

Some Middle Eastern
soups, stews and stuffings
call for the local pungent
dried mint. A tablespoon,
quickly fried in oil and
added just before serving,
imparts a fine fragrance to
certain Turkish dishes.
Sprigs of mint are always
included in the bowls
of herbs and salad served
with *mezze* (hors d'oeuvre).

Indians combine mint with
spices for vegetable and
meat dishes and emphasize
its cooling properties in a
raita of yogurt and mint.
This theme recurs in a cold
cucumber, mint and yogurt
soup of Iran. Further east,
in Vietnam, platters of
mint, basil, dill and rao
ram accompany meatballs
or spring rolls.

At the end of a meal the
clean taste of mint goes
well with fruit and in
chocolate desserts. It has
natural affinities with
fruit cups and punches and,
of course, American
mint julep.

Use fresh or dried
according to the dish. Mint
freezes well, too.

**For key recipes, see pages
56, 78, 109, 115, 124, 129.**

THYME
Thymus species

AN ESSENTIAL FLAVOURING in Western and Middle Eastern cooking, thyme is indigenous to the Mediterranean basin. The thyme that grows wild on the arid hillsides of its native region has infinitely more flavour than that from cooler areas. There are hundreds of varieties of thyme worldwide, each varying somewhat in its aromatic qualities. Middle Eastern zahtar (*Thymbra spicata*) is also often sold as thyme. The two look similar but zahtar's aroma combines thyme, oregano and savory. Use it for grilled meats and in zahtar mixture (see page 131).

DRIED THYME
Dried sprigs from a hot region will have more flavour than those gathered from a northerly garden.

COMMON THYME
T. vulgaris
A cultivated version of wild Mediterranean thyme, it forms a sturdy upright shrub. The basic thyme for the cook.

ORANGE THYME
T. pallasianus
The intense orange aroma makes this thyme suitable for flavouring dessert sauces.

ORANGE-SCENTED THYME
T. citriodorus
'Fragrantissimus'
Use in daubes and stews to which orange peel is added.

GOLD-VARIEGATED THYME
T. 'Doone Valley'
A creeping plant. Its aroma and taste have a lemony note.

CREEPING THYME
T. serpyllum
Milder than common thyme, this grows wild on the dry uplands of central and northern Europe. Use fresh.

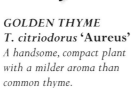

GOLDEN THYME
T. citriodorus 'Aureus'
A handsome, compact plant with a milder aroma than common thyme.

BROAD-LEAVED THYME
T. pulegioides
Use as common thyme, but the flavour is slightly weaker.

LEMON THYME
T. citriodorus
Has an irresistible fresh lemon scent. Use to flavour fish and seafood, roast chicken or veal.

CARAWAY THYME
T. herba-barona
Originally from Corsica, this glossy-leaved thyme has a light caraway note. Use it with meats, poultry, carrots and parsnips and cheese dishes.

VARIEGATED LEMON THYME
T.c. 'Golden Queen'
Pretty plant but with a weaker aroma than lemon thyme. Use for desserts and cream sauces.

SILVER-VARIEGATED THYME
T.v. 'Silver Posie'
Attractive, with silver-edged leaves. Use as common thyme.

AROMA & TASTE
When rubbed, thyme has a fragrant, warm, slightly earthy smell; the taste is warm and piquant with notes of clove, camphor and mint. Dried thyme retains most of its aroma and taste and does not become hay-like.

CULINARY USES
Thyme withstands long, slow cooking, providing a background note with which other flavours blend. It is particularly fine with garlic, onion and red wine, and with basil, bay, lavender, marjoram, parsley and savory.

Indispensable in French cooking, it is used in every stew from *pot au feu* to *cassoulet*. It improves tomato and wine-based sauces, thick vegetable soups, and flavours pâtés, terrines and marinades for pork and game. It is a perfect companion for mushrooms, leeks, aubergines, sweetcorn, tomatoes and pulses. Scatter over roast garlic and grilled vegetables.

In Spain thyme again comes into its own in stews and casseroles, and the custom has passed into Mexican and Latin American cuisines. British cooks put thyme in stuffings, pies, jugged hare and beef stews. Americans use it for clam chowder, but its more important use is as a dried herb in the Creole and Acadian cooking of Louisiana. The Greeks prefer bay and *rigani* (see overleaf) for cooking, but Greek thyme-scented honey is the best in the world.

Use fresh the year round, or it can be dried just before flowering.

For key recipes, see pages 62, 84, 92, 96, 117, 132.

MARJORAM AND OREGANO

Origanum species

THESE CLOSELY RELATED plants have entirely different characteristics for the cook. Sweet marjoram is a fragrant plant that will enhance almost any food. Wild marjoram, *O. vulgare*, a highly variable species, grows from the Himalayas to the British Isles, and in North America. The peppery Mediterranean varieties are commonly called oregano. In Mexico and the Caribbean a number of unrelated plants are also called oregano.

MEXICAN OREGANO
Lippia graveolens
One of the plants commonly known as Mexican oregano (see page 43). Very aromatic, it is often combined with chilli.

GOLDEN MARJORAM
O. vulgare 'Aurea'
A striking plant with dense foliage and white or mauve flowers and a mild aroma.

SMALL-LEAVED OREGANO
O. microphyllum
A native of Crete with the same characteristics as O. vulgare.

WILD MARJORAM
O. vulgare
Innocuous and grassy when grown in cool climates. For flavour, choose a southern subspecies such as hirtum.

GREEK OREGANO
O. vulgare sp.
The most intensely aromatic. Many varieties, cultivated and wild, are sold dried and ground under the Greek name rigani.

POT MARJORAM
O. onites
This has a piquant, bitter note. It is sometimes referred to as Sicilian oregano.

SWEET MARJORAM
O. majorana
Also called knotted marjoram, from the look of the buds, this is a pretty plant. It tastes sweeter than pot marjoram.

CURLED GOLDEN MARJORAM
O.v. 'Aureum Crispum'
Forms a compact plant with crinkled, mild-flavoured leaves.

CRETAN DITTANY
O. dictamnus
The thick silvery leaves – fresh or dried – are mainly used for a tea, but they also flavour meat and vegetable dishes.

CUBAN OREGANO
Plectranthus sp.
Used as oregano in the Caribbean and Mexico, this fleshy succulent has a clean oregano aroma (see page 43).

AROMA & TASTE
Marjoram has a sweet, subtle spiciness; the taste is warm, lightly spicy, bitterish with a note of camphor. Oregano is more robust, with an intense pepperiness and a distinct bite.

CULINARY USES
Marjoram is a highly desirable herb, used in a wide variety of dishes. Its delicate flavour is easily lost in cooking, so add it only at the last moment. Put leaves and flower knots into salads, serve with mozzarella and other young cheeses, and with anchovies, as they do in Italy. It is an ideal flavouring for artichokes, broccoli, courgettes, mushrooms, onions, for eggs and all poultry. With parsley and lemon thyme it makes an excellent stuffing for poultry or fish.

Oregano's penetrating aroma is most obviously associated with Italian cooking, especially tomato sauce, pizza and *pizzaiola* sauce. But its use along the Mediterranean is widespread, and the dried herb is often preferred. In Greece it is used for *souvlaki*, baked fish and Greek salad; in Spain it appears in stews of lamb, chicken or vegetables. Use it for hearty stews, beans, ratatouille, pasta sauces, for marinades and bouquets garnis, flavoured oils and vinegars. The aroma develops with long cooking.

Marjoram dried in bud retains its strength for some months; it also freezes well. Dried oregano retains its strength for a year or more; buy Greek, Italian or Spanish.

For recipes, see pages 113, 114, 116, 120 for marjoram; 62, 92, 100 for oregano.

PARSLEY

Petroselinum crispum

NATIVE TO THE eastern Mediterranean, this biennial herb is used extensively in Western and Middle Eastern cooking. There are curly and flat-leaved varieties, the former most common in northerly climates, the latter throughout southern Europe and the Middle East. Curly parsley is attractive as a garnish, but flat-leaf parsley has the edge when it comes to flavour. Hamburg parsley is grown in central and eastern Europe where it is prized for its edible roots.

AROMA & TASTE

Parsley has a fresh, slightly spicy aroma and a tangy flavour with a light peppery note. The aroma of flat-leaf parsley is finer than that of curly and the flavour stronger and more persistent. Stalks have a more intense flavour than leaves; for long cooking use a bundle of stalks, then remove them and add chopped leaves before serving. The flavour of Hamburg parsley root is somewhere between celeriac and parsley.

CULINARY USES

In Anglo-Saxon cultures parsley has only recently moved beyond being used purely as decoration – "planted like trees in a garden of cold meat", wrote Tom Stobart in *Herbs, Spices and Flavourings* – to being treated as a flavouring.

In French cuisine it is essential in a bouquet garni or mixture of *fines herbes*. Finely chopped leaves are added to savoury butters, a *persillade* (see page 135) or its Catalan equivalent, a *picada* (see page 135). Italians put parsley into stuffings with lemon, breadcrumbs, garlic and capers and into *salsa verde* (see page 139).

In Turkey a parsley omelette heralds spring; in Morocco parsley is served in a salad with onion and lemon, and throughout the Middle East tabbouleh, a salad of cracked wheat and parsley, is a mainstay. Fried sprigs of curly parsley are a delicious garnish for fish, or try it dipped in tempura batter.

Use parsley fresh; it can be frozen for winter use.

For key recipes, see pages 56, 74, 90, 97, 108, 114, 138.

ITALIAN PARSLEY
P.c. 'Italian'
Flat-leaved varieties have a fine flavour and are generally to be preferred for cooking.

FLAT-LEAF PARSLEY
Parsley helps highlight other flavours and is an excellent foil for garlic. It is rich in vitamins A and C, in iron and in calcium.

CURLY PARSLEY
Use for garnishes or to achieve an attractive green colour in a mayonnaise or sauce without a dominant parsley flavour.

MITSUBA (JAPANESE PARSLEY)
Cryptotaenia japonica
This cool climate perennial is an important flavouring in Japan (see page 41).

HAMBURG PARSLEY
P.c. var. tuberosum
Can be grated raw into salads, used to flavour soups and stews or cooked as a root vegetable – it makes a fine purée.

CORIANDER

Coriandrum sativum

PROBABLY THE MOST widely used herb in the world, coriander has long been prized for its flavouring and medicinal properties. It is both herb and spice, for the orange-scented seeds have their own value in savoury and sweet dishes. In China it is known as the "fragrant plant"; there and throughout south-east Asia the leaves and roots are most in demand. In India and the Middle East both leaf and seed are used; and it is the key flavouring, with chillies, in Mexican and Latin American cooking. See also culentro, page 42.

RAO RAM (VIETNAMESE CORIANDER)
Polygonum odoratum
A herb used in Far Eastern cooking (see page 41).

AROMA & TASTE

Leaves and unripe fruits have a distinctive fetid smell which is quite addictive; the flavour is earthy with a suggestion of parsley and mint and a lemony note. The ripe seeds are very different, with a sweet, cedar and sandalwood aroma and a mild, orange peel taste. The roots smell musky and faintly of citrus.

CULINARY USES

Coriander teams with virtually any savoury food; it has particular affinities with garlic, basil, mint, parsley, lemon and lime, chillies and coconut.

India and Mexico both use the excellent combination of coriander and green chillies in chutneys, relishes and salsas. In China it occurs with ginger and spring onions in stir-fried dishes; in Vietnam it is always on the herb and salad plate with basil, dill, mint and rao ram. The roots go into Thai curry paste; the leaves are used with basil, chillies and coconut milk.

In the Middle East its companions are nuts and spices; the seeds and leaves may both be used in the same dish. The Portuguese use coriander with potatoes, broad beans and their excellent clams.

Coriander is superb with fish and seafood, with beans, chickpeas, plantains, rice, root vegetables and squash. It is best added toward the end of cooking to preserve flavour.

Use leaves fresh; roots can be washed, wrapped in paper and refrigerated. Both freeze well.

For key recipes, see pages 60, 68, 87, 90, 120, 138.

LEAVES
These are fan-like and more rounded than flat leaf parsley, although the two are sometimes confused. The smell soon indicates the difference.

ROOTS
More earthy and musky than leaves, roots add depth of flavour. Traditional in Thai curries, try them also in stews and with braised meat or fish.

SEEDS
Ripe seeds are used in curries, vegetables à la grecque, pickles, desserts and cakes; unripe are used in sauces and marinades.

SAGE
Salvia species

A SMALL PERENNIAL bush, sage grows best on the poor dry soils of southern Europe, its native habitat. It is hardy enough to survive in most areas north of the Alps, and is widely cultivated in North America. Aromatic strength varies according to soil and climate.

COMMON SAGE
S. officinalis
There are broad and narrow-leaved varieties, the latter with stunning purplish-blue flowers.

PURPLE SAGE
S.o. **'Purpurea'**
Intensely aromatic but less hardy than common sage.

DRIED SAGE
Has a medicinal, musty smell and is best used for tea.

CLARY SAGE FLOWERS
The flowers of this strongly aromatic biennial make it a handsome plant.

GREEK SAGE
S. fruticosa
More spicy than common sage. Used in Greece to make tea.

CLARY SAGE
S. sclarea
The huge, wrinkled leaves make tasty fritters served with sugar.

PINEAPPLE SAGE
S. elegans
Has a pineapple scent; use with fish, in salads and fruit drinks.

AROMA & TASTE
Sage smells and tastes of camphor, with a note of bitterness and a warm, sometimes burning, spiciness. Its flavour is crude and overpowering to some people.

CULINARY USES
Use fresh sage but use it cautiously. It is best with meats, especially fat meats such as pork, lamb, duck and goose, and strongly flavoured fish.

Its use in Italy is widespread: with liver and veal, in *focaccia*, to make fritters, to flavour polenta. With butter and Parmesan, a few leaves make an excellent pasta sauce. Fried leaves make a good vegetable garnish. In southern France it makes a warming sage and garlic soup; in northern Europe sage accompanies eel and pike; in Britain it is best known in stuffing and in sage Derby cheese.

Sage can be dried but is best used fresh.

For key recipes, see pages 96, 100, 120, 128, 129, 133.

MYRTLE
Myrtus communis

A FRAGRANT EVERGREEN, native to the mountain regions of the Mediterranean basin, myrtle has white flowers and aromatic dark purple berries. In cool climates it needs protection in winter.

MYRTLE SPRIGS
An ornamental bush that deserves to be grown more widely. Put some sprigs on the embers while grilling to perfume food. The compact M.c. subsp. tarentina (near right) is native to Corsica and Sardinia.

AROMA & TASTE
The slightly resinous aroma has similarities with juniper and allspice; the taste is juniper-like and faintly astringent.

CULINARY USES
Used in much the same way as bay. Combine with thyme to flavour meat and game, and with fennel for fish. Discard the leaves on serving. Use for marinades and in pickles. In southern Italy fresh cheeses are wrapped in myrtle leaves to add flavour.

ROSEMARY

Rosmarinus officinalis

THE MOST BEAUTIFUL and aromatic of all herbs, rosemary is a dense evergreen shrub with needle-like leaves and pale blue flowers. It gives off an intense fragrance when touched. Native to the Mediterranean, rosemary thrives in the thin upland soils of southern Europe and grows best by the sea.

WHITE ROSEMARY

Use the attractive white, pink or, more usual, blue flowers as garnishes and in salads.

PINK ROSEMARY

Put rosemary on the barbecue embers when grilling, or use a branch to baste the food on the grill.

BLUE ROSEMARY

The grey-green leaves offset the flowers admirably. Use sprigs that can be removed at the end of cooking to avoid chewing on the spiky leaves.

AROMA & TASTE

The aroma of rosemary is assertive, with notes of camphor and pine, a hint of nutmeg and lavender. Camphor and nutmeg are present in the taste.

CULINARY USES

The favourite herb in Italy, where it is sometimes used to excess. Rosemary combines well with thyme and bay, with garlic and wine. Put a sprig under a roast of pork or lamb, and in marinades for rabbit and game. It goes well with oily fish such as sardines or mackerel, with aubergines, beans, cabbage, courgettes, potatoes and tomatoes.

Rosemary can be dried and crumbled but is better used fresh.

For key recipes, see pages 96, 100, 120, 125, 132.

BAY

Laurus nobilis

NATIVE TO THE eastern Mediterranean, bay trees have long been cultivated in northern Europe. They need a sheltered spot but, should they die back in a very cold winter, the roots will often put out new shoots the following spring.

DRIED LEAVES

Most commonly used in cooking, the aroma is less strong than that of fresh. Keep whole or break into large pieces to remove on serving, or crumble.

FRESH LEAVES

These are more likely to be used in marinades and pickles. When first picked they taste slightly bitter but this fades within a few days.

AROMA & TASTE

Bay has a fresh, sweet balsamic aroma with a spicy note.

CULINARY USES

Basic to much European cooking, bay leaves go into marinades, pickled herrings, Italian vegetables preserved in oil or vinegar, bouquets garnis and *court-bouillons*. They are infused in milk to make béchamel, give a deep flavour to tomato sauce, and perform well with braised meats and in all slow-cooked dishes. Put a leaf and some lemon zest into pears poached in red wine; use bay to give a delicate flavour to creams and custards.

Dry bay leaves in the dark to retain their colour.

For key recipes, see pages 82, 96, 97, 101, 105, 135.

GARLIC AND CHIVES
Allium species

THOUGHT TO BE of central Asian origin, there are some 500 members of the onion family. Most are edible, but not all are good to eat. Many still grow wild, others have been cultivated for thousands of years. The flavours of the onion tribe are perhaps those most taken for granted in the kitchen. After onions, garlic is the most widely used. The Koreans hold the record for consumption per capita, followed by the south-east Asians, then the people around the Mediterranean. This is the home of *aïoli*, *skordalia*, *tarator* and other garlic-based sauces and dressings.

FRESH GARLIC
A. sativum
Young or "wet" garlic is juicy with a gentle flavour. It is excellent braised or roasted whole, alone or with new potatoes.

CHIVES
A. schoenoprasum
The smallest and mildest member of the family. Use fresh, as chives wilt quickly and the aroma fades when cooked.

WELSH ONION
A. fistulosum
Also called oriental bunching onions, these are Asia's largest onion crop. Varieties can have either white or red stems.

ROCAMBOLE (SANDLEEK)
A. sativum var. ophioscordon
Cut the slender leaves (left) as chives, and chop the small bulb (above). Use the tiny cloves that form in the flowerhead as garlic.

DRIED GARLIC
Choose unbruised firm heads;
in winter remove indigestible
green shoots. Use the flat blade
of a knife to crush dried cloves,
a press can give an acrid taste.

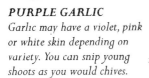

PURPLE GARLIC
Garlic may have a violet, pink
or white skin depending on
variety. You can snip young
shoots as you would chives.

CHIVE FLOWERS
These have a pleasant,
light onion fragrance and
taste, and are attractive
scattered over a salad or
added to omelettes.

CHINESE CHIVES
A. tuberosum
Grown throughout Asia; the
flat leaves and white buds have
a distinctive garlic flavour.
Bud stalks and yellow blanched
leaves are considered a delicacy.

AROMA & TASTE
Chives have a light onion
aroma and spicy onion
flavour. Chinese chives are
more garlicky. The flavour
of Welsh onions lies
between leeks and onions.
Dried garlic is pungent,
hot, sometimes acrid, but
the flavour mellows in
cooking. Rocambole tastes
like a delicate garlic.

CULINARY USES
Scatter chives over soups
and salads, add to egg
dishes, mix with soft cheese
or yogurt, and combine
with parsley, tarragon and
chervil for *fines herbes*.

Chinese chives, cut into
short lengths and quickly
blanched or stir-fried, keep
their colour and flavour.
Use in spring rolls, with
tofu, bean sprouts, eggs,
noodles, and in stir-fried
dishes of beef or prawns.

Both bulbs and tops of
Welsh onions can be used.
Essential for oriental
cooking, they can be
added to western stews,
potato and pulse
dishes shortly before the
end of cooking.

In European cooking,
garlic is roasted
with chicken and
lamb, baked in
wine, puréed,
blanched or
sautéed; raw, it
flavours salads, is rubbed
over bread with tomato
and oil, pounded with egg
yolks and oil to make *aïoli*,
or with nuts and basil to
make pesto. In Asia, its
companions are lemon
grass, fresh ginger,
coriander and chilli.

Wrap Chinese chives and
Welsh onions to prevent
their smell spreading. Keep
garlic in a cool dry place,
not the refrigerator.

For key recipes, see pages
78, 79, 94, 113 for chives;
82, 96, 106, 134 for garlic.

FENNEL
Foeniculum vulgare

NATIVE TO THE Mediterranean basin, but found in most temperate regions, this graceful perennial is one of the oldest cultivated plants. It was one of the herbs Charlemagne decreed in 812 should be grown on all the imperial estates. All parts are edible.

GREEN FENNEL
Use stalks and leaves to flavour court-bouillon and marinades for fish. Snip leaves with scissors; do not chop.

BRONZE FENNEL
The reddish fronds blend handsomely with the green in a garden border. It has a milder aroma and flavour.

SEEDS
The seeds contain a high proportion of anethole, which accounts for the similarity of flavour with anise, but they are more astringent.

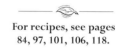

AROMA & TASTE
Fennel has a warm anise-liquorice aroma and taste with a slight sweetness and a hint of camphor.

CULINARY USES
A traditional flavouring for fish; early cookery books recommend serving fennel sauce with oily fish. In Provence, red mullet, bream and bass are grilled or baked with fresh or dried stalks. It is essential to Sicilian *pasta con le sarde* and has affinities with rice, lentils, potatoes, cabbage and beetroot. The Italians roast pork with the seed and use it to flavour *finocchiona*, the renowned salami of Florence.

Leaves are best fresh; dried stalks keep for a season.

For recipes, see pages 84, 97, 101, 106, 118.

CHERVIL
Anthriscus cerefolium

"SWEET CHERVIL IS so like in taste unto Anis seede that it much delighteth the taste among other herbs in a sallet" (Parkinson, *Paradisus*, 1629). Much appreciated in France, Germany and Holland, its arrival in the markets signals springtime and chervil soup and sauces appear on menus. Elsewhere it deserves to be better known.

AROMA & TASTE
The smell is sweet, the taste soothing; both are a subtle blend of anise, tarragon and caraway. Chervil brings out the flavours of other herbs, most clearly in the classic *fines herbes* blend with parsley, tarragon and chives.

CULINARY USES
Chervil has affinities with eggs, fish, poultry, veal, green beans, carrots mushrooms and potatoes. Use lavishly and add it toward the end of cooking as the aroma and flavour dissipate quickly. Chervil gives a delicate taste to vinaigrettes and sauces.

Use fresh, although it can be frozen for a few weeks. All flavour fades if dried.

For recipes, see pages 74, 78, 79, 90, 106, 116.

LEAVES
Chervil is easy to grow in the garden from seed. Pick outer leaves first, the inner ones will keep on growing. The lacy foliage fades to pale cream and pink as it dies off.

ANISE

Pimpinella anisum

ANISE HAS BEEN cultivated for centuries. Our ancestors grew it for its digestive properties; in medieval times, anise comfits (sugar-coated seeds) were taken after rich meals; in India today the seeds are chewed to aid digestion and freshen the breath. Anethole oil from the seeds is used in anise-flavoured aperitifs and liqueurs.

SEEDS
The seeds give a spicy note to breads and desserts, and can be used in marinades for seafood and in sauces. Commercially, they are used in confectionery.

LEAVES
Anise has fine, feathery leaves with clusters of white flowers in late summer. It can be grown from seed quite easily and plants are sometimes available from herb farms.

AROMA & TASTE
Anise, the strongest of the anise-type herbs, has a refined liquorice-like aroma and taste with sweet, mildly peppery undertones.

CULINARY USES
Use young anise leaves in salads, and chopped leaves and young stalks to flavour carrots, parsnips, pumpkin and chestnuts, or to make tea. A mixture of leaves and seeds makes a fresh flavouring for rich meats such as pork and duck. Anise-flavoured drinks such as pastis and anís are well worth keeping in the kitchen to enliven fish, shellfish and vegetable dishes.

Use fresh leaves only; seeds are used dried.

For recipes, see pages 79, 115.

DILL

Anethum graveolens

DILL HAS BEEN grown for its leaves and seeds since antiquity. In the Middle Ages it was held to be a magic herb that would guard against witchcraft. Indigenous to central Asia and southern Europe, its main producers today are Scandinavia, Poland, Russia, Turkey and Italy.

SEEDS
The seeds are used in cakes and breads, soups and stews, and for pickling. Pickled cucumbers, or dill pickles, are favourites in many countries.

LEAVES
Dill loses its fine aroma in cooking, so is best added at the last moment. Snip rather than chop the leaves.

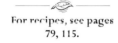

AROMA & TASTE
Dill leaves have a fragrant anise-like aroma with a lemony note; the flavour is of anise, mild but sustained. The seeds smell rather like caraway; the taste is warm and slightly sharp.

CULINARY USES
The fresh, clean taste marries well with fish and seafood, especially salmon. It enhances scrambled or baked eggs and makes a fine salad with cucumber and soured cream. In Greece, dill is added to spinach; in Turkey and the Middle East it flavours courgettes, potatoes, broad beans and rice.

Best fresh, but freezes well. Dried has little aroma or flavour.

For recipes, see pages 52, 54, 76, 104, 109, 120.

ANGELICA

Angelica archangelica

PROBABLY NATIVE to the Middle East, but for centuries grown even in far northern Europe, angelica is a vigorous, handsome biennial which grows up to 2m (7ft). It makes a showy plant with its bright green serrated leaves and huge domes of tiny, pale yellow-green flowers. All parts are aromatic and edible.

AROMA & TASTE

A crushed leaf gives off a pleasantly sweet, musky scent. The overall taste is again musky with a warm aftertaste, but the young stalks and leaves can also be bittersweet and sharp.

CULINARY USES

Young, juicy stems can be eaten fresh or boiled as a vegetable. Chopped young leaves can be added sparingly to salads, to a young white cheese or used to stuff fish. Leaves stewed with rhubarb reduce its acidity. Oil distilled from the seeds and roots is used to flavour vermouths and liqueurs of the Benedictine type.

Use fresh angelica; dried leaves have a much reduced flavour.

For recipes, see pages 79, 115, 116.

DRIED LEAVES
The leaves may be dried and used in baking and for making a herbal tea, but little remains of the aroma or flavour of fresh angelica leaves.

STALKS
France has long had an important industry in candying young angelica stalks, but these are becoming increasingly difficult to buy.

CELERY

Apium graveolens

WILD CELERY, or smallage, is a common European plant from which cultivated celery was developed. By 1800, three kinds were known: garden celery, with fleshy white or green stems, round-rooted celeriac, and cutting celery, closest in appearance to wild celery.

AROMA & TASTE
The taste of cutting and Chinese celery is warm yet somewhat rank and bitter, but it mellows with cooking. Water celery is milder, reminiscent of both celery and parsley.

CULINARY USES
Seldom eaten raw, celery is added to many soups and stews, often along with celeriac. In China, leaves and stalks are used in soups, vegetable dishes and stir-fries. In Vietnam, finely chopped water celery is used raw to flavour salads, or briefly cooked and added to soups and fish or chicken dishes. In Japan it is also used for *sukiyaki*.

Use fresh celery only.

For recipes, see pages 106, 112.

CUTTING CELERY
Used as a flavouring herb in northern Europe the year round. It looks very like flat-leaf parsley; only smelling it reveals the difference.

WATER CELERY
Oenanthe stolonifera
Also called water dropwort and Vietnamese celery. The young shoots are most prized in winter in south-east Asia and Japan.

CHINESE CELERY
Chinese celery (kun choi) looks similar to cutting celery; it is widely grown in China and used as a vegetable and as a flavouring herb.

CARAWAY
Carum carvi

CARAWAY HAS BEEN cultivated throughout Europe since medieval times; it is native to northern and central Europe and Asia. Today Holland, Germany, Poland and Russia are the main producers, but it is also an important crop in Canada and the United States. All parts of the plant are edible but, commercially, caraway is grown for its seeds.

AROMA & TASTE
The aroma combines elements of dill, anise and cumin with a note of lemon. The taste is similar, warming and slightly bitter. The seeds have the strongest flavour.

CULINARY USES
Caraway combines well with parsley and thyme. In central European and Jewish cooking, the seeds are put into soups, cabbage, sauerkraut and potato dishes; Hungarians add them to goulash, Germans and Austrians to meat stews. Caraway is used to flavour cheeses, sausages, breads, especially dark rye breads, and cakes. The liqueur Kümmel is flavoured with caraway.

Use the leaves fresh.

For recipes, see pages 79, 115.

SEEDS
These are crescent-shaped with tapering ends. In Alsace a small dish of seeds is traditionally served with the local Münster cheese.

LEAVES
Caraway's delicate fern-like leaves make a pleasant addition to salads or fresh white cheeses and can serve as a garnish for vegetables.

LOVAGE
Levisticum officinale

A NATIVE OF SOUTHERN Europe, lovage is a tall, stately perennial with hollow stalks, large shiny toothed leaves and greenish-white flowers. All parts are aromatic and edible. Lovage is easy to grow and deserves to be better known. It is strongly flavoured so needs to be used sparingly, although its pungency diminishes in cooking.

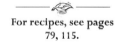

AROMA & TASTE
There is some similarity with celery, but lovage is more piquant and has musky overtones with notes of anise, lemon and yeast. Dishes flavoured with lovage need less salt.

CULINARY USES
Lovage seems to give body to dishes; it is particularly good with rice, pulses and vegetables. It makes an excellent soup and its flavour goes well with smoked fish. Try lovage butter with potatoes or shred a few leaves into a tomato or egg dish. The blanched stalks can be eaten as a vegetable, dressed with a vinaigrette.

Fresh leaves are best. Seeds may be dried.

For recipes, see pages 74, 115, 116, 138.

SEEDS
Lovage seeds dry well. They have a sweeter flavour than the leaves and are useful for adding to breads, pickles, sauces and marinades.

LEAVES
These are used fresh or blanched in salads and for sauces, stuffings and stews. They can be dried, but the taste is more intensely yeasty.

HORSERADISH

Armoracia rusticana

HORSERADISH IS EASILY recognizable by its large wrinkled leaves, which grow straight up from the root, and in summer by its white flower spike. It can be invasive if not dug up regularly. Indigenous to eastern Europe, it has long been appreciated in the cooking of Russia, Scandinavia and central Europe. It also serves as the bitter herb among the symbolic foods of Passover.

AROMA & TASTE

Extremely pungent when grated, but this dissipates rapidly, so prepare just before eating. The taste is sharply mustardy. If cooked, the volatile oils are driven off and so no pungency develops.

CULINARY USES

Grated, it can be put into beetroot and potato salads. It is more usually blended with cream, vinegar and sugar to make a sauce, and is the first condiment offered with roast beef. In Germany it accompanies ox tongue. It combines well with mustard and with chives. Serve, too, with oily fish.

It will keep for 2–3 weeks in the refrigerator and can also be grated and frozen.

For a recipe, see page 79.

ROOT
This is scrubbed and grated, but fresh horseradish is not easy to buy. Dried flaked root is better than most of the over-sweetened preparations on sale.

LEAVES
The leaves are pungent when crushed. Although it is normally the root that is eaten, a few tender young leaves can be used to give a sharp taste to a salad.

CURRY PLANT

Helichrysum italicum

THIS DECORATIVE PERENNIAL, a native of southern Europe, will grow up to 60cm (24in) in a sunny position. The silver-grey downy leaves and bright yellow flowers set off the green plants of the herb garden. It gives off a warm spicy smell when rubbed.

AROMA & TASTE

When crushed, the plant has a distinct scent of curry with a hint of sweetness. The taste is less aromatic. The flowers have a similar, milder fragrance.

CULINARY USES

Never used for curry, in spite of its name, and only used straight from the plant. A sprig or two of curry plant added to thick vegetable soups, to lamb and pork stews, to rice and to pickles will give them an elusive and subtle spicy flavour. Remove the sprig before serving.

Curry plant leaves should be used fresh.

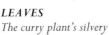

LEAVES
The curry plant's silvery needle-like leaves and shrubby habit make it a handsome edging in a formal garden.

FENUGREEK

Trigonella foenum-graecum

NATIVE TO THE eastern Mediterranean, the plant's botanical name, *foenum-graecum*, means Greek hay. A good source of vitamins, proteins and minerals, fenugreek is useful in a vegetarian diet. The seeds are used as a spice in the Middle East and in India, where they are a constituent of curry powder.

SEEDS
The strongly aromatic seeds can be sprouted. Use these shoots raw in small quantities in salads or steam or stir-fry.

LEAVES
This robust annual is easy to grow in mild climates and is a good addition to the herb garden. Picked fresh, the leaves are excellent in salads.

AROMA & TASTE
Fresh fenugreek is mildly pungent and slightly bitter. Aroma and taste are intensified in the dried leaves, and there is a fragrant hint of hay.

CULINARY USES
The bitter flavour of the leaves is much loved in India where they are cooked with potatoes and with spinach and other greens, or chopped and added to the dough for *chapatis* or *puris*. In Iran, fenugreek leaves, fresh or dried, are used in herb stews and flavourings for meat.

Use fresh from the garden, or buy dried leaves from Indian or Iranian shops. The Indian name is *methi*, the Iranian *shamba-lileh*.

For recipes, see pages 79, 96, 108, 133.

MUSTARD

Brassica juncea

MUSTARD SEEDS ARE perhaps the most important temperate-climate spice crop, and several varieties of leaf are eaten as a vegetable in China and the southern United States. However, mustard is generally only considered to have potential as a herb in central Europe.

SEEDS
Brown mustard seeds are the kind most used for commercial mustard production. They can also be crushed and used in herb oil and vinegar dressings.

LEAVES
The mustard plant has dark green leaves, the larger ones toothed like rocket. The seed pods that follow the small yellow flowers are smooth or hairy depending on variety.

AROMA & TASTE
The leaves have distinct pungency and a warm peppery taste; the yellow flowers have a mild mustard flavour.

CULINARY USES
The young leaves make a fine addition to green salads; different varieties of mustard seedlings — purple, green and beautiful, feathery Japanese mizuna — are grown commercially for salad mixtures. They are also easy to raise in the garden.

Shredded leaves make a pleasant garnish for beetroot, carrots, celeriac, courgettes, potato and tomato salads. Add them to a ham or beef sandwich or to a dish of stir-fried vegetables.

Use fresh leaves only.

BORAGE
Borago officinalis

AN ANNUAL OF southern European origin, borage thrives on chalky soils throughout Europe and North America. In the past it was held to make people cheerful and courageous; research has now shown that it stimulates the adrenal glands.

FLOWERS
These look marvellous floating on a creamy soup or in a salad. They can also be crystallized in syrup to use for desserts.

LEAVES
Shred the coarse prickly leaves unless they are being used as an aromatic garnish.

AROMA & TASTE
Borage has a light aroma and stronger taste of cucumber; it is slightly tart, cool and fresh.

CULINARY USES
Shred young leaves for salads (especially with cucumber), dressings, sauces and salsas. Borage combines well with yogurt, soured cream and fresh white cheeses. Add to soups in the last few minutes if served warm. In northern Italy it is sautéed and used with spinach and other herbs in risottos and pasta fillings. Among the herbs, team it with anise, burnet, dill, garlic. Use in fruit, alcohol or yogurt-based summer drinks.

Use borage sparingly and always fresh.

For recipes, see pages 73, 108, 115.

LEMON VERBENA
Aloysia triphylla

LEMON VERBENA IS a half-hardy shrub, native to South America. Brought to Europe in the 17th century, it was much planted in Mediterranean gardens. Its intense fragrance was soon taken up in the manufacture of toilet waters; its culinary career came later, first as a tea, then as an alternative to lemon juice.

LEAVES
The narrow, rough-textured leaves are tough to chew on, so chop them finely or remove before serving. Dried leaves are only good for tea, and fresh would be better.

AROMA & TASTE
Lemon verbena has an enticing aroma of fresh, sharp lemon. The taste is less strong, but the aroma is long-lived.

CULINARY USES
It is excellent with fish and poultry – put some sprigs into the cavity of a fish or chicken; add it to stuffing for pork. Try it in a pilaf with lemon zest and toasted pine nuts, or with carrots, mushrooms or squash. Combine it with lemon thyme or balm. It makes a fresh-scented sorbet or ice-cream, and can be chopped for fruit tarts and desserts. A few leaves flavour a jar of sugar.

Lemon verbena leaves can be frozen.

For recipes, see pages 79, 122, 125, 129, 136.

FRENCH TARRAGON
Artemisia dracunculus

FROM ITS NATIVE habitat of western Asia, where it is used with great enthusiasm by Georgian cooks, tarragon reached Europe with the Moors. As classic French cooking developed in the 17th century, it became a key flavouring. Its finest uses are still in the French tradition.

LEAVES
Tarragon's aroma develops in cooking, but can easily annihilate other flavours: use carefully, and it will enhance other herbs.

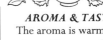

AROMA & TASTE
The aroma is warm and spicy, with notes of anise and a hint of hay; the taste is refined, yet firm, with a light touch of pepper and anise, warm and subtle, but penetrating.

CULINARY USES
Indispensable in *fines herbes*, tarragon flavours many classic French sauces — *béarnaise, ravigote, gribiche, tartare*. It makes one of the best herb vinegars and lifts mustard to another realm. Use it with eggs, chicken, rabbit, crab, lobster, scallops, asparagus, leeks, avocado, mushrooms, salsifies, in tomato salad.

Fresh tarragon is best but it also freezes well. Use only French, not Russian tarragon.

For recipes, see pages 66, 90, 101, 105, 106, 125.

SOUTHERNWOOD
Artemisia abrotanus

ONE OF THE PRETTIEST aromatic small shrubs, southernwood, as its name implies, is native to the Middle East and southern Europe. It has a quite delicate scent of lemon and pine, with a medicinal background note. Use the young, tender shoots for cooking.

LEAVES
A fine bitter citrus flavouring for beef, pork, salmon, eel and mackerel. Use with lemon thyme or balm to bring out the citrus element.

MUGWORT
Artemisia vulgaris

MUGWORT GROWS WILD through much of Europe and Asia. It aids the digestion of fat and is used primarily with pork, duck and goose — in Germany, where it is widely cultivated, it is known as 'goose herb'. In Asia it is boiled or stir-fried.

LEAVES
The aroma, which develops during cooking, is of juniper and pepper, with a note of mint and mild bitterness. Mugwort keeps its strength dried, when flower shoots are used.

CALAMINT
Calamintha species

CALAMINT, OR MOUNTAIN BALM, grows wild in southern Europe and western Asia. Used for perfumes, pharmaceuticals and in the production of liqueurs, it also has a reputation as a culinary herb in southern European cuisines. Its sweetly peppery and minty aroma deserves more attention from cooks elsewhere.

COMMON CALAMINT
C. officinalis
Calamint is an attractive perennial with lilac-purple flowers and velvety leaves.

GARDEN CALAMINT
C. grandiflora
This has pink flowers and larger, slightly drooping leaves; there is also a variegated form.

AROMA & TASTE
The whole herb is aromatic with notes of thyme, mint, camphor and a suggestion of tangerine peel; the taste is moderately pungent, warm and lightly peppery.

CULINARY USES
Treat calamint as a milder form of mint. Use it to flavour grilled fish, roast lamb, all forms of game, and in marinades, stuffings or sauces. Its peppery notes combine well with aubergines, all types of bean, lentils, mushrooms, potatoes and tomatoes.

Calamint is used dried for making tea; for cooking, use fresh shoots and young leaves.

For recipes, see pages 97, 114.

CATMINT AND CATNIP
Nepeta species

WIDELY GROWN IN temperate regions, these pretty herbs are sweetly aromatic with notes of mint and camphor. Cooks can benefit from their slightly sharp flavour in salads, soups, sauces, with pork and duck.

CATMINT
N. racemosa
Catmint's leaves are downy and the flowers blue to lavender and long-lasting.

CATNIP
N. cataria
Catnip is usually more aromatic than catmint; it has white or pink flowers.

For recipes, see pages 97, 139.

MOUNTAIN MINT
Pycnanthemum pilosum

NATIVE TO northern America, mountain mint is a graceful plant with pink flowers, reddish stalks and narrow leaves that look somewhat like savory.

LEAVES
Use the shoots and young leaves of mountain mint as a mint substitute, but sparingly. It has a distinctive mint aroma with a strong menthol component. The taste is minty with bitter notes.

SUMMER AND WINTER SAVORY

Satureja species

BEFORE SPICES REACHED Europe, savory was one of the strongest flavourings available. Native to the Caucasus and eastern Mediterranean, it has been used for 2000 years. Its warm peppery aroma is appreciated around the Black Sea and in southern Europe, notably in Provence. Summer and winter savory can replace each other, but adjust the quantities.

AROMA & TASTE
Summer savory is the more subtle; pleasantly piquant with similarities to marjoram and thyme. The aroma of winter savory is more assertive, with an additional note of pine; the taste more penetrating.

CULINARY USES
Known as the bean herb (for its anti-flatulent properties as well as its aromatic character), summer savory suits green and broad beans, winter savory is more satisfying with the haricot tribe. Use summer savory in salads and with mackerel, carp, pike, chicken and pigeon. Winter savory suits meat and game dishes, stews and gratins.

Use both types fresh.

**For recipes, see pages
91, 94, 102, 106, 109, 116.**

**SUMMER SAVORY
S. hortensis**
An annual garden herb with soft grey-green leaves, summer savory enhances vegetables. Try it with aubergines, onions, peas, peppers, tomatoes and beans.

**WINTER SAVORY
S. montana**
A perennial evergreen with rather tough leaves. Use sprigs and remove before serving.

THYME-LEAVED SAVORY

Satureja thymbra

NATIVE TO SARDINIA, Crete and Greece, this creeping plant is not hardy in cool climates. Its aroma has notes of thyme, mint and savory; the taste is closer to savory with a pleasant bite.

LEAVES
Thyme-leaved savory can be used in the same way as winter savory or thyme, in slow-cooked soups and stews, especially with meat or game.

MICROMERIA

Micromeria species

MICROMERIA IS native to southern Europe. It is warmly aromatic, with notes of thyme and savory. In Balkan cooking it is used like thyme; the Italians use it in pasta sauces, omelettes, with fresh cheeses and poultry.

EMPEROR'S MINT
Micromeria thymifolia *has the finest aroma; emperor's mint, the species more often found in Britain, is coarser with a bitterish mint taste.*

HYSSOP
Hyssopus officinalis

THIS COMPACT DECORATIVE perennial is native to southern Europe, southern Russia and North Africa. It is hardy, easy to grow and, as an evergreen, is available to the cook all year round. It has a long history as a culinary, cleansing and medicinal herb; its volatile oil is used in the preparation of liqueurs.

LEAVES
An attractive plant and good addition to the culinary repertoire. Fresh or dried leaves can be used for tea.

FLOWERS
The bright blue, pink or white aromatic flowers can be used in cooking. They also attract bees.

AROMA & TASTE
Hyssop's aroma is difficult to define: camphor refined by savory and lavender, with a hint of rosemary. Its slightly bitter taste combines elements of these with slight mintiness.

CULINARY USES
The flavour is strong, so use hyssop sparingly. It combines well with parsley, chervil, bay, thyme, mint, and is good with rich meats – pork, lamb, kid, venison. Chopped young leaves and flowers go well in green salads, with the cabbage tribe and with dishes of beans and lentils. It also has an affinity with plums and apricots.

Hyssop dries well; harvest it when just in flower.

For recipes, see pages 105, 115, 116, 120.

AGASTACHE
Agastache species

THE AGASTACHES ARE native to North America. Anise hyssop is starting to find some popularity in Europe now, and this erect showy herb, with its spikes of lilac flowers, is a handsome addition to a sunny part of the garden and well worth the cook's attention.

ANISE HYSSOP
A. foeniculum
The light green leaves provide an elusive anise note when used in salads. In the US it is grown for honey.

AROMA & TASTE
Both leaves and flowers of anise hyssop smell lightly of anise and liquorice; the taste is sweetly anise. Mexican hyssop is minty.

CULINARY USES
Anise hyssop can be used to flavour fish and shellfish dishes and sauces to serve with them. It combines well with green beans, tomatoes, courgettes and young beetroot. Add just before the end of cooking. Its sweetness also makes it a good companion to fruit; try a little in place of the tarragon in the pear and raspberry salad (page 113). Add finely chopped leaves to cream cheese and garnish with the flowers.

Anise hyssop can be frozen but is not worth drying.

For recipes, see pages 79, 115, 116.

MEXICAN HYSSOP
A. mexicana
Sometimes called giant hyssop, this variety grows wild in Mexico where the leaves and flowers are used to make tea.

BERGAMOT
Monarda didyma

POPULARLY CALLED bergamot, bee balm, Oswego tea or horsemint, the genus is named for Nicolas Monardes, a Spanish physician whose *Joyfull Newes out of the Newe Founde Worlde* (translated Frampton, 1577) was the first American herbal. This stately hardy perennial, with its bright mopheads of flowers, is native to America. In the 18th century seeds were brought to Britain.

FLOWERS
The purple, red or pink flowers are the most fragrant part of the plant, and add a dramatic splash of colour to a green or fruit salad.

BERGAMOT TEA
Early settlers along the north-eastern seaboard of America found the Indians made a tea from the plant and adopted the habit.

AROMA & TASTE
Flowers and leaves have a distinctive citrus aroma and taste, ranging from lemon to orange according to the variety.

CULINARY USES
Add leaves to duck and chicken dishes, and use them in omelettes, salsas and sauces. Use the flowers in salads and with fruit: the citrus flavour has a particular affinity with melon, strawberries, papaya and kiwi fruit. Bergamot tea is good, and if you add a couple of flowerheads to a pot of Indian tea it will have a fine scented aroma and flavour.

Use fresh flowers and leaves for cooking; dried may be used for tea.

For recipes, see pages 79, 115, 129.

LEMON BALM
Melissa officinalis

A PERENNIAL, native to southern Europe, lemon balm is not a showy plant. It has the characteristic square stems of the mint family, crinkled light green leaves and small white flowers.

VARIEGATED BALM
M.o. 'Aurea'
More compact and less hardy than ordinary balm, this makes a brilliant splash in the border and the salad bowl.

PLAIN-LEAVED BALM
Balm makes one of the best tisanes, but use a generous amount because it loses its aroma in hot water. Dried leaves can be used for tea.

AROMA & TASTE
Crushed leaves yield a fresh and persistent lemon aroma; the flavour is sweet and subtly lemon-scented with a note of mint.

CULINARY USES
Balm is excellent with poultry and fish, in stuffings, marinades and sauces, and makes a delicate herb butter and fine vinegar. Tear young leaves for salads. They team well with virtually any steamed or sautéed vegetable, with rice and cracked wheat. Use shredded leaves with lemon zest as a garnish. Add balm to custards, ice-creams, desserts and cakes.

Fresh is best but it freezes well for 2–3 months.

For recipes, see pages 93, 124, 129.

SCENTED GERANIUMS
Pelargonium species

SCENTED GERANIUMS reached Europe in the 17th century from the Cape of Good Hope. In the 19th century the French perfume industry discovered their oil in place of attar of roses and geranium growing boomed.

AROMA & TASTE
There are some 200 aromatic varieties. Some have fruit aromas – lemon, orange, apple; some are spicy – clove, cinnamon, nutmeg; others have the scent of flowers or woodland – rose, pine. Rose and lemon are the two most widely used in the kitchen.

CULINARY USES
Infuse the leaves in cream, milk, wine or syrup and use the liquid to flavour ices, custards, other desserts and cakes. Leaves put in the bottom of a cake tin will impart a subtle flavour. Add leaves for the last few minutes when making jam or jelly.

Use fresh leaves.

For recipes, see pages 124, 125.

P. crispum 'Variegatum'
An upright shrubby plant with crimped leaves that are freshly lemon-scented.

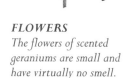

FLOWERS
The flowers of scented geraniums are small and have virtually no smell.

P. 'Graveolens'
Rose-scented with a hint of spice, reminiscent of rosewater or Turkish delight.

P. crispum 'Prince of Orange'
This low, compact geranium has a sweet orange scent.

P. 'Attar of Roses'
Aptly named, this has a sweet concentrated rose perfume and pale pink flowers. Use a leaf or two to scent a jar of sugar, as you would a vanilla pod.

COSTMARY
Tanacetum balsamita

"THESE PLANTS grow everywhere in gardens, and are cherished for their sweet floures and leaves," wrote Gerard in 1633. Today costmary is something of a rarity. It can look straggly, but has the advantage that it persists into winter.

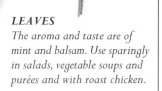

LEAVES
The aroma and taste are of mint and balsam. Use sparingly in salads, vegetable soups and purées and with roast chicken.

For a recipe, see page 96.

RUE
Ruta graveolens

NATIVE TO southern Europe, rue is a handsome evergreen with soft bluish-green leaves and bright yellow flowers. A bitter herb with an assertive aroma, the taste is spicy and sharp. Use with caution; large amounts can be toxic.

VARIEGATED RUE
Variegated is used as plain. Add rue to a mix of basil, mint, oregano, parsley, savory and thyme to use in place of salt.

For recipes, see pages 115, 134.

PLAIN-LEAVED RUE
Use a leaf or two in salads, herb stuffings, vegetable soups, cheese dishes; also in marinades for game and herb vinegars.

SWEET CICELY
Myrrhis odorata

INDIGENOUS TO northern Europe, sweet cicely, or anise chervil, is a graceful perennial with light green, fern-like leaves. Slow growing, it will eventually reach 1m (3ft) in height and width. It blooms early, bearing white flowers in spring, and by midsummer has umbrella-like seedheads.

SEEDS
These taste almost better than the leaves. Green seeds add a spicy note and nutty texture to salads; use ripe, black seeds for desserts.

LEAVES
A natural sweetener, the leaves reduce the tartness of other foods. The flavour has particular affinities with apricots, peaches and nectarines.

AROMA & TASTE
The leaves and seeds have a musky aroma and taste of anise with a note of lovage and a decided sweetness.

CULINARY USES
Leaves and ripe seeds can flavour cakes, fruit pies, cream cheese or sweet cream sauces. Leaves give a subtle flavour to omelettes, salads or a clear oriental-style chicken soup, and bring out the sweetness of root vegetables and squash. Stir chopped leaves into a purée of carrots, parsnips or pumpkin.

Use as soon as possible after cutting as the leaves wilt quickly.

For recipes, see pages 83, 116, 120, 122.

WOODRUFF
Galium odoratum

THIS PRETTY creeping plant's scent is faint when fresh, but cutting releases the heady aroma of new-mown hay. This remains when the sprigs are dried or frozen and is readily transferred to liquids.

LEAVES
Woodruff has affinities with melon, pears and apples. Add to grape or apple juice. A syrup is used to flavour desserts, creams and cakes. Infuse in marinades and dressings.

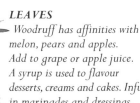

For recipes, see pages 125, 129.

MARSH MALLOW
Althaea officinalis

ONCE GROWN widely for its medicinal and culinary properties, marsh mallow is now rather neglected. An attractive perennial, it has a light musky smell and sweet taste.

LEAVES AND FLOWERS
Use in salads; they go well with fennel. Leaves are stir-fried or steamed. Marsh mallow sweets were once made from the roots.

SEEDS
Add these to marinades and salad dressings and to breads.

For a recipe, see page 115.

ORIENTAL HERBS

During the last ten years several oriental herbs have become popular in the West, with the spread of Thai restaurants and the development of East-West and Pacific Rim cuisines. Each year a few more plants arrive in specialist nurseries – there was a noticeable increase after travel began again to Vietnam, where fresh herbs are part of every meal. Many deserve to be more widely known.

SANSHO

Zanthoxylum piperitum

IN JAPAN *kinome*, sprigs of young leaves of the sansho or prickly ash tree, are picked as a herb. Only used fresh, their season is limited and they are not easy to find in the West.

DRIED BERRIES
The ground powder is sprinkled on fatty foods, and is one of the seven ingredients of shichimi, used as a table condiment.

LEAVES
Crush leaves lightly to release the aroma; try them in clear soups and with salads.

AROMA & TASTE
The taste is delicately minty.

CULINARY USES
Kinome sprigs are used as a garnish for soups, tofu, seafood and grilled meats. Add chopped leaves to dressings for Japanese and western salads, especially of raw root vegetables. Sansho berries are ground to a tangy powder which has a slightly numbing sensation in the mouth.

The sprigs keep for a few days in the refrigerator.

PERILLA

Perilla frutescens

NATIVE TO CHINA, perilla has long been grown in Japan. Also called *shiso* and beefsteak plant (the red variety), leaves are sometimes sold in oriental shops, and the sprouts in supermarkets. It also grows easily in the garden or in a pot.

RED PERILLA
In Japan this is mostly pickled (sold in vacuum packs). Use big fresh leaves to wrap poultry or fish for steaming or braising.

GREEN PERILLA
A useful and attractive addition to the herb garden; shred leaves for soups and salads, fresh white cheeses and herb butter.

AROMA & TASTE
Green perilla is sweetly aromatic, with notes of anise, cinnamon and lemon. Red is faintly musty with notes of coriander leaf and cinnamon.

CULINARY USES
Leaves and seeds are eaten with *sushi* and *sashimi* (perilla counteracts parasites in raw fish). Chopped leaves make an excellent flavouring for rice and pasta, salmon, sea bass and turbot. Fry whole leaves in tempura batter.

For recipes, see pages 86, 114.

LEMON GRASS
Cymbopogon citratus

THIS TALL PALE green grass is native to tropical Asia. It is now cultivated in Australia and Florida and has become widely available. It will flourish in cooler climates if it is overwintered indoors. The lemon rind perfume, with a hint of sweetness, gives a fresh subtle fragrance to cooking from Indonesia to Vietnam. It blends harmoniously with chilli, garlic and shallots, with coriander and oriental varieties of basil.

STALKS
Remove outer leaves and use only the bulbous bottom parts of the stalks, the rest is very fibrous. Very freshly cut stems show purplish rings.

AROMA & TASTE
The clean lemon aroma is echoed in the taste, a blend of lemon and lime, subtle but sustained.

CULINARY USES
Use the bottom part of the stalks; crush them to put in marinades or the steaming water for fish and chicken. Chop coarsely and pound for Thai curry pastes. Slice finely for soups and stir-fries.

Lemon grass enhances the flavour of fish, seafood, chicken, beef and pork; also broccoli, cabbage, aubergines and mushrooms.

Keep for 2–3 weeks in the refrigerator or 2–3 months in the freezer. Dried, as stalks or powdered, it lacks the clean taste of fresh.

For recipes, see pages 60, 72, 88.

KAFFIR LIME LEAVES
Citrus hystrix

THE LEAVES AND RIND of the fruit of this evergreen tree are responsible for the light tangy edge to Thai and Indonesian dishes. In the West it has become easier to buy fresh leaves (and sometimes the wrinkled knobbly fruits) as well as dried leaves and rind, or pickled rind, from oriental shops.

LEAVES
These grow as two on a single petiole; use fresh leaves when possible, dried are a less fragrant substitute.

AROMA & TASTE
Kaffir lime has a floral-citrus aroma, similar to lemon verbena, delicate yet assertive. The rind is strongly citrus and slightly bitter.

CULINARY USES
Both zest and leaves are used in soups, curries and stir-fries. Soak dried strips of rind in warm water first. Shredded leaves are sometimes used as a garnish but they are tough to chew on. I prefer to cook with whole leaves and remove them. Add a couple of leaves to a western stew or casserole instead of bay for an elusive citrus flavour.

Leaves keep for 2–3 weeks in the refrigerator and freeze well.

For recipes, see pages 60, 72.

CURRY LEAVES
Murraya koenigii

THE LEAVES — called *meetha neem* in India — of a small tree that grows wild throughout the sub-continent but is also cultivated in Indian gardens for its attractive foliage and for culinary purposes. Curry leaves are a daily essential in southern Indian and Sri Lankan cooking. Buy them, preferably fresh, from Indian shops and some supermarkets.

LEAVES
Put a spray of leaves into western dishes to give a light curry note. Dried have little flavour; it takes 2–3 times as many to give the aroma and flavour of a fresh sprig.

AROMA & TASTE
When bruised, curry leaves give off a curry-like scent with a citrus note. The taste is warm, bitterish and pleasant.

CULINARY USES
In southern India and Sri Lanka fresh sprigs are fried with spices, put into simmering meat, vegetable and fish dishes (to be removed at serving), chopped into fresh chutneys, and ground for spice mixtures. They are an essential ingredient of south Indian curry powder. Try them in the aromatic oil — the *tadka* — that flavours the lentil dish on page 105.

Keep leaves in the refrigerator for a week or two, or freeze.

For a recipe, see page 88.

CHINESE BOXTHORN
Lycium barbarum

ALSO CALLED matrimony vine, boxthorn is grown for food in Asia and as an ornamental in Europe. The leaves are peppery and mint-like.

LEAVES
In China boxthorn is used as a pot herb and for soup, traditionally with pork or pig's liver. Try adding the leaves to western soups and stews, but cook them briefly.

BERRIES
These have a liquorice-like flavour when ripe; use them in meat stews. Dried berries are sold as wolfberries.

SPICE BUSH
Elscholtzia stauntonii

THIS SMALL temperate-climate shrub, also called mint bush, has toothed leaves which turn red in autumn and purplish-pink flowers. Its sweet aroma of caraway and anise is echoed in the taste, with hints of mint and lemon.

LEAVES
Stir the chopped leaves into mashed potato, vegetable purées or a cream sauce for game; you can also add them to a green salad.

MITSUBA
Cryptotaenia japonica

IN JAPAN, MITSUBA leaves and stalks are used to season soups, fish and vegetable dishes and savoury custards. It is cooked very briefly to preserve its flavour. Small bundles of stalks are often tied in knots just below the leaves and fried for tempura or used as a garnish.

LEAVES
The flavour of mitsuba has elements of parsley and angelica, a hint of clove and something of the sharpness of sorrel; it is distinctive, restrained and agreeable.

For a recipe, see page 86.

RAO RAM
Polygonum odoratum

VARIOUSLY CALLED Vietnamese coriander, parsley or mint, rao ram has an intensified aroma of coriander with peppery citrus notes. In south-east Asia it is usually eaten raw as a salad or herb accompaniment, but it remains aromatic when lightly cooked. A great discovery, and well worth seeking out. Use as coriander.

LEAVES
P. odoratum has oval leaves with purplish markings; the related P. foetidum with longer, plain green leaves and a nasty rank aroma and taste should be avoided.

For recipes, see pages 94, 97, 112.

PANDANUS
Pandanus odoratissimus

THE MUSKY new-mown hay aroma of pandanus (screwpine) is a common flavouring for south-east Asian desserts. Infuse leaves in cream or milk to give western puddings a subtly exotic fragrance.

LEAVES
Combined with coconut, the flavour of pandanus is delicious. Leaves go into pilafs; Indian kewra essence, which is distilled from the flowers, scents syrups and sweets.

For a recipe, see page 88.

VAP CA
Houttuynia cordata

A PERENNIAL water-loving plant, much used on herb platters in Vietnam and neighbouring countries. Crushed leaves have a mild lemony yet catty aroma; the taste is pleasantly sourish.

LEAVES
Use chopped leaves to flavour simmered or braised dishes of fish or pork. Shred leaves into a clear oriental-style soup. Some varieties have a rank smell; test before buying.

HERBS FROM THE AMERICAS

Many Mediterranean and other European herbs were taken to the Americas by colonists. Now some of the indigenous herbs are making their way on to the world market as demand has grown with greater awareness of the culinary traditions of Mexico and South America. Some of these are uniquely American plants, but others are also found in tropical Asia.

CULENTRO

Eryngium foetidum

ALSO CALLED *cilentro* and *cilantrón,* this herb is used in Caribbean and Central American cooking and in south-east Asia (where it is *ngó gai* to the Vietnamese). It is related to coriander, but more pungent. Buy it from Thai shops.

LEAVES
The long serrated leaves are prickly and tough; dried leaves are said to keep their flavour better in long cooking.

AROMA & TASTE
The fetid element of coriander is more pronounced in culentro; the taste is earthy and pungent.

CULINARY USES
Use the leaves as coriander but with restraint. In Mexico and the Caribbean it flavours stews, soups and salsas. In south-east Asia it goes into curries and soups. Combine with lemon grass and mint to give soups and sauces a sourish flavour.

EPAZOTE

Chenopodium ambrosioides

CONSIDERED PRIMARILY as a Mexican herb, its use spreads across the northern countries of South America. It combines well with chillies, coriander and oregano – the main flavourings of the region.

LEAVES
Epazote grows easily and is often found as a weed in North America, but in cooler conditions it is less aromatic.

AROMA & TASTE
Epazote smells sharply camphorous; the taste is pungent, bitterish and citrus, and it is quite addictive.

CULINARY USES
In Mexico it is essential for black bean dishes and for *quesadillas* (cheese-filled tortillas). Young leaves are cooked as pot herbs; it flavours pork, crab cakes, fish, corn and squash.

For recipes, see pages 68, 87.

MEXICAN OREGANO
Lippia, Poliomintha and other genera

THE NAME OREGANO is given to several unrelated plants that smell and taste somewhat like oregano. *Poliomintha longiflora* has narrow leaves similar to summer savory; other oreganos belong to the Monarda genus; Cuban and Puerto Rican oreganos are succulents (see page 17). Use with chillies and other herbs to flavour meats, beans and vegetable stews or try them instead of Mediterranean oregano in other dishes.

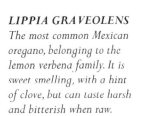

LIPPIA GRAVEOLENS
The most common Mexican oregano, belonging to the lemon verbena family. It is sweet smelling, with a hint of clove, but can taste harsh and bitterish when raw.

MINT MARIGOLD
Tagetes lucida

ALSO CALLED winter tarragon, the Mexican name *yerbanis* seems more accurate for the aroma is delicately anise-like with a hint of mint. Mint-scented marigold leaves and flowers are excellent in salads, the leaves enhance fish and shellfish, eggs, tomatoes and avocados. Use them for vinegar and add chopped leaves to sauces.

LEAVES
Both the leaves and golden marigold flowers, in late summer, are scented. Used extensively in south-west USA.

SASSAFRAS
Sassafras albidum

AN ORNAMENTAL North American tree with aromatic leaves, formerly used medicinally and as a tea, the roots to flavour root beer, and the oil to cure toothache. It is now known that safrole, a constituent of sassafras oil, is a carcinogen. Safrole is not present in the dried leaves.

FILE POWDER
Filé powder may be made only of dried sassafras leaves or may have dried thyme, oregano or bay added to it.

AROMA & TASTE
The young leaves are dried and ground to make filé powder, which smells and tastes sourish, rather like lemony sorrel with notes of tea. The flavours are enhanced by brief heating.

CULINARY USES
Filé powder is a key ingredient, probably taken over from the local Indians, in the cooking of Louisiana, where it is used to flavour and thicken gumbos.

Gumbo, a Cajun soup, contains vegetables, fish or seafood or a variety of meats and is served with rice. The filé powder is added at the end of cooking. Try it in similar soups and stews.

SALAD HERBS

A salad without herbs tends to be bland and dull. Those shown here are mostly used whole, mixed generously with other leaves, but a tablespoon or two of chopped herbs will flavour a salad. Be sure to balance the pungent with the milder herbs.

ROCKET

Eruca vesicaria ssp. *sativa*

NATIVE TO western Asia and southern Europe, rocket is naturalized in North America, where it is known by its Italian name, arugula. A popular herb until the 18th century, when it almost disappeared in northern Europe, it is now enjoying a well-deserved revival.

LEAVES
Rocket has toothed leaves and small white or yellow flowers. It is easy to grow, especially in partial shade.

TURKISH ROCKET
Bunias orientalis
Grows wild in parts of Asia; it has a sharper flavour, rather like horseradish.

AROMA & TASTE
Rocket has a warm, peppery smell; the taste is pleasantly pungent. The piquant edible flowers have a faint orange aroma.

CULINARY USES
Whole leaves can be added to any composed salad, or make a fine flavoured salad on their own, especially with a nut oil dressing. Rocket and new potato salad is good. Shredded leaves can be used for herb butter or in a herb dressing for pasta.

Use fresh; do not freeze.

For recipes, see pages 83, 113, 115.

SORREL

Rumex acetosa

GARDEN SORREL GROWS easily throughout the temperate zones. French sorrel prefers the drier climate of the Mediterranean. Both are high in vitamin C and folic acid, the latter giving the sour taste.

FRENCH SORREL
Rumex scutatus
French or buckler leaf sorrel is finer and more succulent than garden sorrel, with a lemony note.

WOOD SORREL
Oxalis acetosella
Although unrelated, this has a similar taste, and is refreshing in salads and summer drinks.

GARDEN SORREL
Use young leaves in salads; treat older ones as spinach. Cooked in butter, it combines with spinach or chard.

AROMA & TASTE
Sorrel has little aroma but a tart sharp taste, with a hint of lemon.

CULINARY USES
Use leaves whole or shredded. It makes a fine soup with a sour, refreshing tang. Sorrel purée balances the richness of duck and pork, goes well with eggs and, finished with cream or egg yolk, makes a good sauce for fish.

Use fresh, although cooked sorrel can be frozen.

For recipes, see pages 72, 78, 90, 108, 116, 139.

WINTER PURSLANE
Montia perfoliata

ALSO KNOWN AS claytonia, this hardy but delicate-looking annual has a mild fresh flavour. It is a useful salad herb the year round, but is especially welcome in autumn and winter.

LEAVES
Both winter and summer purslane combine well with broad beans, beetroot and new potatoes.

SUMMER PURSLANE
Portulaca oleracea

THE FLESHY LEAVES are crunchy and refreshing. A standard ingredient of Middle Eastern *fattoush* and Provençal *mesclun*, purslane has affinities with chervil, burnet and the cresses.

LEAVES
Produces several crops if shoots are harvested regularly. Bundles can often be bought in Middle Eastern and Greek shops.

For recipes, see pages
83, 112, 115.

DANDELION
Taraxacum officinale

USE THE BITTER but appetizing young leaves in spring salads. They are also good combined with new potatoes, pieces of crisp bacon and a garlicky or walnut oil dressing.

LEAVES
These can be made more tender by blanching them under a flower pot. Cultivated blanched dandelions look very similar to curly endive.

For recipes, see pages
113, 115.

SALAD BURNET
Sanguisorba minor

BURNET IS COOL and astringent, reminiscent of cucumber. Use young leaves for green salads and in sauces, in mixtures of *fines herbes* and to blend into cream cheese.

LEAVES
Burnet is seldom found for sale as a cut herb but it makes an attractive garden plant, often lasting well into winter. Always use fresh leaves.

For recipes, see pages
79, 84, 91, 115, 136.

EDIBLE FLOWERS

Flowers are being rediscovered as food, a fragrant link to the past, when dozens were gathered for the kitchen. Violet wine, flower puddings, lavender conserve, pickled marigolds were not culinary exotica but part of the normal diet, at least of the well-to-do.

MARIGOLDS

Calendula officinalis and *Tagetes patula*

IN ANCIENT TIMES the pot marigold was valued for its edible qualities in India, the Arab lands and by the Greeks. Parkinson noted its "pretty strong and resinous sweet sent", that leaves and flowers were used as a pot herb, and the flowers for possets, broths and drinks.

POT MARIGOLD
C. officinalis
Marigold petals can be dried in a very low oven and then ground.

FRENCH MARIGOLD
T. patula
The flavour of these petals, dried, blends well with cinnamon and cloves.

AROMA & TASTE
Both marigolds have a musky aroma and a lightly bitter, musky taste.

CULINARY USES
Dried marigold petals have long been used in Europe as poor man's saffron to colour rice and other dishes; in Georgia they are an essential flavouring, used in spice mixtures and with chilli pepper, garlic, walnuts. Georgians prefer French marigolds. Fresh petals can also be used in salads and desserts after removing the bitter white heel. See also page 43.

For a recipe, see page 115.

NASTURTIUMS

Tropaeolum majus

THE CONQUISTADORS brought nasturtiums from Peru to Europe in the 16th century. They combine well with parsley, tarragon, burnet and chives. The seeds can be pickled.

SEEDS
Soak seeds in salted water for 24 hours; strain. Boil enough white wine vinegar to cover them. Cool and pour over the seeds. Leave for 6 months.

FLOWERS
These make a fine vinegar with some white peppercorns and mace (see page 136).

LEAVES
Add young leaves, shredded or whole, to a mushroom and bean salad (see page 112), with a dash of pastis in the dressing.

AROMA & TASTE
Leaves and flowers taste peppery, rather like watercress. The flowers are sweeter.

CULINARY USES
Young leaves are good in sandwiches and salads. The flowers look pretty in green salads. Scatter them over new potatoes or haricot beans or stir them into a risotto. Sliced leaves and flowers put into a vegetable soup for the last few minutes give an agreeable pepperiness.

For recipes, see pages 112, 113, 115.

ROSES
Rosa species

OLD COOKERY BOOKS abound with recipes for rose conserves, pickled rosebuds, tarts and sauces of hips. Roses were appreciated for their fragrance and sweet flavour as much as their beauty. Any highly scented varieties can be used for cooking.

ROSE PRESERVES
Use roses to make jam and to flavour syrups and vinegars.

OLD ROSES
Varieties of Rosa gallica *(left and right),* R. damascena *and* R. centifolia *are the most fragrant.*

ROSE PETALS
When using petals, cut out the white heel at the base, rinse briefly and pat dry. Try adding them to salads containing fruit.

AROMA & TASTE
The more scented the rose, the more flavour it has. Deep red roses have a special appeal.

CULINARY USES
Chop petals into a bowl of raspberries and thick cream or add to other fruit desserts. Use dried buds to flavour a stew in the Moghul manner. Rosewater, still used today in Middle Eastern cooking, gives a delicate fragrance to meat dishes, cakes and creams.

Rose petals can be dried and powdered; dried buds are used for tea.

LAVENDER
Lavandula species

LAVENDER IS NOT commonly associated with the kitchen but, used carefully, it gives a heady yet elusive flavour. Infuse leaves or flowers in cream for ices and other desserts. Add to braised rabbit or chicken, or even when cooking rice.

LEAVES
Fresh lavender is as strongly aromatic as rosemary so use it lightly; dried is stronger still and is best avoided.

FLOWERS
Both flowers and leaves can be used, but flowers are more aromatic. Use whole sprigs for lavender vinegar; flowers are best for flavouring sugar.

For recipes, see pages
124, 125, 129.

VIOLETS AND VIOLAS
Viola species

OF THE HUNDREDS of violet varieties only a few are fragrant. The flowers make very pretty salads with endive or chervil, a delicate filling for an omelette or garnish for a cold soup. Violet water is a forgotten flavouring for cakes and puddings.

VIOLA TRICOLOR
Candy flowers in syrup or frost them with egg white and icing sugar to decorate desserts.

VIOLA ODORATA
This smells and tastes the sweetest, but it does not last: "The perfume and suppliance of a minute," said Shakespeare.

For recipes, see pages
113, 115, 125, 136.

CLASSIC DISHES

This section features traditional dishes from many countries, showing the great variety in the use of herbs in different cultures. Most of these recipes use fresh herbs, alone or in combination with other flavourings. Coriander is used in nearly all the major cuisines, parsley throughout the western ones. Other herbs, such as tarragon and lemon grass, are more particularly associated with one area or tradition.

All the recipes serve 4, unless otherwise indicated.

SOUPE AU PISTOU

Vegetable soup with pistou

This substantial soup from Provence is served with pistou, the local version of Genoese pesto. The vegetables may vary, but squash or pumpkin, some root vegetables and beans are always used. The soup is almost better reheated, but make the pistou at the last moment. Serves 6.

Green beans

Bouquet garni

Haricot beans

Squash

Potatoes

Turnips

Carrots

Onion

INGREDIENTS

2 litres (3½ pints) water
1 large onion, chopped
3 carrots, diced
2 small turnips, diced
4 potatoes, diced
250g (8oz) squash or pumpkin, diced
150g (5oz) haricot beans, soaked and
boiled for 10–15 minutes
bouquet garni made up of bay leaves and sprigs of
parsley, thyme and sage, tied together
150g (5oz) green beans, cut into short lengths
3 courgettes, diced or quartered
75g (2½oz) short macaroni or pasta shells
300g (10oz) tomatoes, skinned and chopped
salt and black pepper

Pistou
large handful of basil leaves
3 cloves garlic
coarse salt and black pepper
60g (2oz) freshly grated Parmesan
approximately 8 tbsp (120ml) olive oil

PREPARATION

1 Bring the water, lightly salted, to the boil and add the onion, carrots, turnips, potatoes, squash, haricot beans and bouquet garni. Reduce the heat and simmer, covered, for about 30 minutes or until the vegetables are just beginning to soften.
2 Add the green beans, courgettes, macaroni and tomatoes and simmer for a further 15 minutes or so, until the pasta is cooked but is still *al dente*.
3 To prepare the pistou, tear the basil leaves and pound them with the garlic, salt and pepper in a mortar. Add the Parmesan gradually, alternating it with spoonfuls of olive oil, to make a thick paste. You may find this easier to mix with a large fork than with a pestle. Continue until all the cheese and oil have been amalgamated.
4 Season the soup to taste with salt and pepper before serving and remove the bouquet garni. The pistou should not be heated, but served separately as an accompaniment. Stir it well first as the oil has a tendency to separate from the rest of the sauce.

Tomatoes

Basil

Garlic

Salt

Black pepper

Parmesan

Olive oil

Macaroni

Courgettes

GRAVAD LAX

Scandinavian salmon marinated with dill

An elegant dish that is simple to prepare. The dill imparts a delicate taste to the salmon and the slight sweetness of the sauce balances it well. Mackerel and trout can be prepared in the same way, but salt them only for the shorter suggested time. Serves 8–10.

INGREDIENTS

2kg (4lb) salmon, preferably a middle cut
100g (3½oz) sea salt
75g (2½oz) sugar
1 tbsp white peppercorns, crushed
2 large bunches dill, chopped

Mustard Sauce
3 tbsp Dijon mustard
½ tsp powdered mustard
1 tbsp sugar
3 tbsp lemon juice
75ml (2½fl oz) sunflower or other neutral oil
4 tbsp chopped dill

PREPARATION

1 Scrape away all the scales from the salmon with the back of a knife, but leave the skin on. Slit the fish open along the backbone and take this out. Check both fillets for bones and remove them. You may find a pair of tweezers useful for this.

2 Combine the salt with the sugar and white pepper and rub the mixture well into the flesh of each piece.

3 Scatter a third of the dill over the bottom of a shallow dish just large enough to hold the salmon. Put in one piece of fish, skin side down, and cover this with another third of the dill. Put the other half of the salmon on top, flesh side down, and strew over the rest of the dill.

4 Cover the dish with clingfilm, then place a weighted board on top and leave in the refrigerator for at least 36, and preferably 48, hours. Turn the fish once during this time and baste it with any brine that collects in the dish.

5 Just before you are about to serve the salmon, combine the two mustards with the sugar, lemon juice and oil to make the sauce. Whisk together thoroughly and, when they are well blended, stir in the dill.

6 Drain the fish and scrape off the dill and spices, then slice it thinly on the slant and serve with the mustard sauce and bread or new potatoes. The salmon will keep in the refrigerator for up to a week, although it will start to dry out.

Dill

White peppercorns

Sugar

Sea salt

Salmon

Dijon
mustard

Powdered
mustard

Lemon
juice

Sunflower
oil

TURKISH COURGETTE PANCAKES

These simple pancakes, called *mücver*, are always a great success whether served hot as a vegetable course or part of a vegetarian meal, or cold for a picnic or buffet. The Turks sometimes use finely diced aubergine and a little green pepper and tomato instead of courgettes to make the pancakes.

INGREDIENTS

6–7 tbsp olive or sunflower oil
2 large onions, grated
3 courgettes, grated
100g (3½oz) white cheese, such as feta,
grated or crumbled
5 tbsp chopped dill
5 tbsp chopped flat-leaf parsley
4 tbsp sifted plain flour
3 eggs
salt and black pepper
sprigs of dill or parsley, to garnish

PREPARATION

1 Heat a tablespoon of oil in a frying pan and lightly fry the onion until golden.

2 Squeeze the excess moisture from the grated courgettes by pressing them in a colander or sieve or squeeze them in your hand. Add them to the pan and fry over a high heat for 2–3 minutes. Put to one side.

3 Whisk the cheese, dill, parsley, flour and eggs together in a large bowl. Season, but check on the saltiness of the cheese before adding more salt.

4 Pour the contents of the frying pan into the cheese and eggs and mix well.

5 Wipe out the pan and add the remaining 5–6 tablespoons of oil, enough to shallow fry the pancakes. When thoroughly hot, drop in tablespoons of the mixture one by one to make small pancakes. Leave room for them to spread a little. Cook until they are golden brown on both sides. Do not try to turn the pancakes until the undersides are sufficiently browned or they may fall apart.

6 Drain off any excess oil on kitchen paper and serve the pancakes garnished with a few sprigs of dill or parsley. The pancakes can be eaten hot, warm or cold. A tomato salad or a bowl of garlic-flavoured yogurt makes a good accompaniment.

Dill

Feta cheese

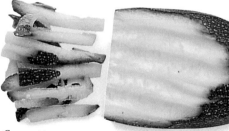

Courgettes

Onions

Olive oil

Flat-leaf parsley

Flour

Eggs

Salt

*Black
pepper*

TABBOULEH
Bulgar wheat and herb salad

A traditional Lebanese salad, also popular in neighbouring countries. Proportions of bulgar wheat to herbs and tomatoes vary, but it is essential that the wheat plays only a background role. The salad should be predominantly green and red, with specks of cream, and taste vibrantly of parsley and lemon. Tabbouleh is served as part of *mezze* (hors d'oeuvre) in the Middle East.

INGREDIENTS

60g (2oz) bulgar wheat
4–5 spring onions, finely chopped
500g (1lb) ripe tomatoes, skinned, deseeded and chopped, with the juice reserved
2 large bunches flat-leaf parsley, total weight approximately 350g (11½oz), leaves chopped
5 tbsp chopped mint leaves
8 tbsp olive oil
juice of 1 lemon, or more to taste
salt and black pepper
½ tsp ground allspice
1 lettuce, preferably cos or other firm variety

PREPARATION

1 Leave the bulgar wheat to soak in a bowl of cold water for 20 minutes, until soft and swollen. You can check whether it is sufficiently tender by nibbling a grain or two. If not, leave for a few minutes longer. Drain in a sieve and press out any excess water.

2 Add the spring onions and tomatoes, with as much of their juice as possible. Stir in the parsley and mint. The best way to mix the salad is with your hands.

3 Make a dressing by whisking together the oil, lemon juice, salt, pepper and allspice – the salad should have quite a tart, lemony flavour. Stir the dressing into the tabbouleh and let it stand for 30 minutes or so at room temperature before serving, so that the flavours have time to blend.

4 To serve, line a platter with the lettuce leaves and use them to scoop up the tabbouleh, which is piled in the centre of the dish. An assortment of raw vegetables, such as spring onions, radishes, carrots and cucumbers cut into wedge-shaped batons, makes a good accompaniment.

Mint

Flat-leaf parsley

Tomatoes

Spring onions

Bulgar wheat

Olive
oil

Lemon juice

Salt

Black
pepper

Ground
allspice

Lettuce

SALADS

The judicious addition of fresh herb leaves can transform a few simple ingredients into a memorable salad. Depending on their characteristics, you can use herbs to add a mild, subtle flavour or a more dominant note, but always take care to balance the tastes and textures of the salad.

MANGO, MINT AND PRAWN SALAD

Refreshing and light, the mint, lime juice and garam masala give a sharp, clean taste to the creamy dressing. Serve as a first course.
See page 115 for recipe.

RED PEPPER SALAD WITH OLIVES AND ANCHOVIES

Coriander is usually associated with oriental or South American food, but its pungent, lemony taste combines well with the traditional Mediterranean flavours of roasted red peppers, olives and anchovies.
See page 115 for recipe.

DAIKON AND KIWI FRUIT SALAD

Inspired by Japanese cuisine, this salad combines the spicy-sweet flavour of basil or perilla with the crisp texture of the oriental radish and refreshing kiwi fruit.
See page 114 for recipe.

BROAD BEAN SALAD WITH PARMA HAM

A combination of summer beans, Parma ham and sweet tomatoes is finished with a generous scattering of marjoram.
See page 114 for recipe.

HERB AND FLOWER SALAD

Refreshing in colour and flavour, this delicate tangle of green leafy herbs is garnished with violas and nasturtiums to make a tempting display.
See page 115 for recipe.

THAI VEGETABLE CURRY

All the ingredients for this curry can be found in Thai and oriental shops, many in supermarkets. If you have to use substitutes, it will lack subtlety, although the flavour will be good. You can use fewer chillies, but this quantity gives depth of flavour rather than excessive heat.

INGREDIENTS

250ml (8 fl oz) thick coconut milk
500ml (17 fl oz) thin coconut milk
200g (7oz) green or yard-long beans, cut in short lengths
3 courgettes, thickly sliced and quartered
200g (7oz) broccoli florets
250g (8oz) canned bamboo shoots, sliced
6 kaffir lime leaves (if unavailable, use lemon grass or grated lime or lemon rind)
10 small white aubergines, quartered
3–4 tbsp fish sauce

Green Curry Paste

2 stalks lemon grass, lower part only, thinly sliced
6 thin slices galangal (if unavailable, use fresh ginger)
1 tsp chopped kaffir lime peel
2 tbsp chopped coriander root (if unavailable, use leaves)
5 shallots, chopped
3 cloves garlic, crushed
1 tsp shrimp paste (or a dash of fish sauce)
½ tsp coriander seeds, roasted
½ tsp cumin seeds, roasted
10–15 birdseye or other small green chillies, or to taste
20g (¾oz) Thai or sweet basil leaves
To garnish: holy basil leaves and 1 large green chilli, finely sliced

PREPARATION

1 Mix 100g (3½oz) creamed coconut with 175ml (6fl oz) water for thick milk, and 75g (2½oz) with 400ml (14fl oz) water for thin. If using canned milk, chill the cans first to separate thick and thin.
2 Pound the curry paste ingredients with a pestle and mortar or blend in a processor until smooth.
3 Heat the thick coconut milk in a wok and stir in the curry paste. Cook for about 10 minutes, stirring frequently, until the oil starts to seep out.
4 Add the beans and courgettes and toss for a few minutes. Pour in the thin coconut milk and bring to the boil, then add the broccoli, bamboo shoots and kaffir lime leaves and cook until the beans have almost softened. Add the aubergines and simmer until soft, about 5–8 minutes more.
5 Season with fish sauce, remove from the heat and discard the kaffir lime leaves. Scatter over the torn holy basil and green chilli. Serve with rice.

Fish sauce

White aubergines

Kaffir lime leaves

Bamboo shoots

Broccoli

Courgettes

Green beans

Creamed coconut

Garlic

Cumin seeds

Green
chilli

Kaffir
lime peel

Coriander
root

Shallots

Shrimp
paste

Coriander
seeds

Birdseye
chillies

Basil

Galangal

Holy
basil

Lemon grass

CREOLE JAMBALAYA

This highly seasoned rice dish is always started with that trinity of Louisiana ingredients, onion, celery and green pepper, and invariably uses dried herbs. Jambalaya varies according to the cook and the ingredients to hand, but a mixture of seafood and meat is common.

INGREDIENTS

30g (1oz) butter or 2 tbsp sunflower oil
1 large chicken breast, cubed
200g (7oz) ham, preferably smoked, chopped
1 onion, chopped
2 sticks celery, sliced
1 green pepper, deseeded and diced
2 spring onions, chopped
3 cloves garlic, chopped
2 bay leaves, crushed
1½ tsp dried thyme
1 tsp dried oregano
5 fresh sage leaves, shredded
4 tbsp chopped flat-leaf parsley
3 large tomatoes, skinned and chopped
600ml (1 pint) chicken stock or water
salt
½ tsp black pepper
½ tsp cayenne
200g (7oz) long-grain rice
20 tiger prawns or large shrimps, cooked and peeled

PREPARATION

1 Heat the butter or oil in a large heavy pan, add the chicken and ham and cook slowly for about 5–6 minutes, stirring frequently, until browned.
2 Add the onion, celery and green pepper and let them start to brown before adding the spring onions, garlic, bay leaves, thyme, oregano, sage and half the parsley. Cook for 5 minutes, stirring and scraping the bottom of the pan if necessary.
3 Put in the tomatoes and stock, and season with salt, if necessary, black pepper and cayenne.
4 When the liquid comes to the boil, stir in the rice. Let it come back to the boil, cover and reduce the heat. Simmer for 20–25 minutes until the rice is tender, but still has a bite.
5 Add the prawns, distributing them evenly through the mixture, and simmer, uncovered, for 5–10 minutes until they are heated through. It will probably help to stir with a wooden fork during this last stage of the cooking, to keep the rice grains separate.
6 Check the seasoning and stir in the remaining parsley. Serve hot.

Sage leaves

Dried oregano

Bay leaves

Garlic

Spring onions

Green pepper

Celery

Onion

Butter

Smoked ham

Chicken breast

Cayenne

Salt

Black
pepper

Long-grain
rice

Prawns

Chicken stock

Tomatoes

Flat-leaf
parsley

Dried
thyme

MEAT DISHES

Herbs such as rosemary, oregano and thyme, which are high in aromatic oils and can withstand heat, are the best to use with meat, when high temperatures or long cooking are needed. Simple grills can be quickly finished with a *persillade*, a mixture of parsley and garlic, or a herb butter, see pages 135–36.

PORK NOISETTES WITH FENNEL

Although it is more often associated with fish, fennel is an excellent herb for flavouring braised pork.
See page 101 for recipe.

GRILLED STEAK WITH BEARNAISE SAUCE

This classic French combination is easy to prepare as long as you do not hurry the sauce making. Tarragon, an essential herb for many French sauces, gives béarnaise a fine, pure flavour.
See page 101 for recipe.

SALTIMBOCCA ALLA ROMANA

A simple dish that can be made in a matter of minutes. The combination of veal, Parma ham and sage is a great Italian favourite.
See page 100 for recipe.

ARISTA ALLA FIORENTINA

*Rosemary is the traditional
Italian herb for pork. In this
dish it is combined with
garlic and cloves to season
a finely flavoured roast.*
See page 100 for recipe.

LAMB KLEFTIKO

*A Greek recipe that gives
extra succulence to the meat.
The pungency of the oregano
is mellowed in these slowly
cooked parcels of lean lamb.*
See page 100 for recipe.

CHICKEN WITH TARRAGON

Chicken with tarragon is a classic of French bourgeois cooking. Simple to prepare, it has a delicate, yet distinct, flavour of tarragon. Serve the chicken with rice or boiled potatoes, spinach, glazed carrots, mangetouts or young broad beans. The leftover stock will make a well-flavoured soup. Serves 6.

INGREDIENTS

30g (1oz) butter
3 carrots, finely sliced
2 onions, finely sliced
1 stick celery, finely sliced
1¼ litres (3 pints) chicken stock
1 chicken, weighing approximately 1.5kg (3lb)
250ml (8fl oz) dry white wine
small bunch tarragon
salt and black pepper
1 egg yolk
100ml (3½fl oz) crème fraîche
1 tsp flour

PREPARATION

1 Heat the butter in a pan large enough to hold the chicken. Add the carrots, onions and celery and cook gently, with the lid on, until they are softened but do not let them brown.

2 In a separate pan, heat the stock until warm.

3 Add the chicken to the vegetables, placing it breast up, and pour over the stock and wine. There should be enough liquid to cover the chicken – if necessary add a little water. Bring to the boil over a moderate heat and skim off any scum that rises to the surface.

4 Reserve 3 tablespoons of tarragon leaves for the sauce and add the rest to the pan. Season with salt and pepper.

5 Cover tightly and let the chicken poach for about an hour. The stock should just shudder, not bubble. Check to see if the bird is cooked by inserting the point of a knife where the thigh joins the body – there should be no trace of blood. When it is ready, remove the chicken, taking care to drain it well when you lift it from the pan, carve it and keep warm while you make the sauce.

6 Strain the stock, pour 400ml (14fl oz) into a pan and boil to reduce it by half. Beat the egg yolk with the crème fraîche and flour. Remove the stock from the heat and stir in the egg mixture to make a smooth, creamy sauce. Then add the reserved, finely chopped, tarragon leaves. Serve the sauce separately.

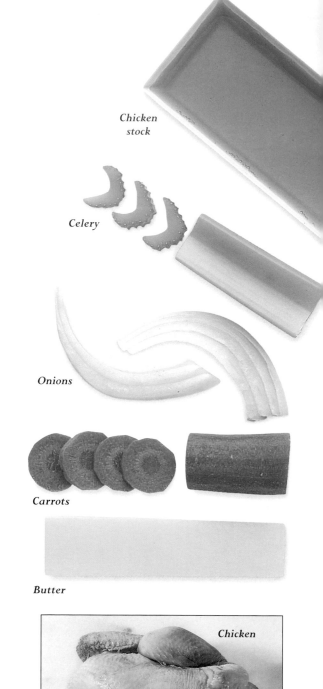

Chicken stock

Celery

Onions

Carrots

Butter

Chicken

Tarragon

Salt

Black pepper

Crème fraîche

Egg yolk

Flour

Dry white wine

DUCK WITH MOLE VERDE

The appetizing green colour of the sauce, or *mole verde*, in this classic Mexican dish comes from the blend of pumpkin seeds, herbs and tomatillos, a light green, tart fruit in a papery husk. The dish is based on a recipe in Diana Kennedy's *The Cuisines of Mexico*.

INGREDIENTS

4 duck breasts
Mole Verde
100g (3½oz) pumpkin seeds
6 tomatillos, fresh or canned
4 serrano chillies, chopped and deseeded
2 cloves garlic, crushed
1 small onion, chopped
6 cos lettuce leaves, torn
1 bunch watercress or radish tops
3 tbsp chopped coriander
leaves from 3 sprigs fresh epazote, or approximately 1 tbsp dried
good pinch of ground cumin
black pepper
2 tbsp sunflower or groundnut oil
250ml (7fl oz) chicken stock

PREPARATION

1 To make the mole verde, dry-roast the pumpkin seeds in a frying pan for 4–5 minutes, stirring so that they do not colour too much or burn. Set aside to cool, then grind them.

2 Blend the tomatillos in a food processor with the chillies, garlic, onion, lettuce leaves, watercress, coriander, epazote, cumin and pepper. (If you are using fresh tomatillos, first remove the husks and cut the flesh into chunks.)

3 Heat the oil in a pan and cook the sauce over a high heat so that it thickens, stirring from time to time. It will take about 5 minutes. Set aside.

4 Stir the pumpkin seeds into the stock, or liquidize the two together, and add to the sauce.

5 Heat a heavy frying pan and put in the duck breasts, skin side down. Cook them in their own fat for 10 minutes, turn once and cook for 5 more minutes. They should remain slightly pink.

6 While the duck is cooking, very gently heat the sauce, making sure that it does not boil or it will lose its greenness. Let it barely simmer for 15 minutes, stirring regularly.

7 Lift the duck from the pan, remove all the fat and slice the meat. Spoon the sauce on to a serving platter, arrange the slices of duck on top and serve with tortillas.

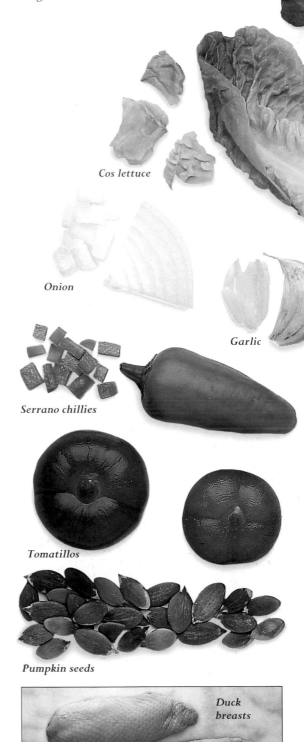

Cos lettuce

Onion

Garlic

Serrano chillies

Tomatillos

Pumpkin seeds

Duck breasts

Watercress

Coriander

Epazote

Ground cumin

Black pepper

Chicken stock

Sunflower oil

RECIPES

*This part of the book contains a selection of dishes
from around the world in which herbs play an
important part. Sometimes their use is wholly
traditional, but many of the recipes include unusual
varieties or, in some cases, familiar herbs are used in
unexpected ways. The different flavours that can be
produced may, I hope, encourage you to develop
your own ideas into successful experiments.*

All the recipes serve 4, unless otherwise indicated.

SOUPS, STARTERS AND EGG DISHES

Herbs whet the appetite. In the Middle East a bowl of aromatic leaves and salad greens always accompanies the assortment of dips, salads, little pies and vegetable dishes that make up the *mezze* at the beginning of a meal. Herb soups such as chervil or cucumber and borage make an elegant first course; more hearty combinations with vegetables can make a meal in themselves.

SCALLOP AND HERB SOUP

I first encountered this soup at the Thai Cooking School at the Oriental Hotel in Bangkok and the recipe is based on theirs. Reduce the number of chillies if you prefer your food less fiery. Extra lime juice can replace the tamarind if necessary.

INGREDIENTS

300g (10oz) scallops
2 x 400ml (14fl oz) cans of coconut milk
2 stalks lemon grass, lower part only, finely sliced
4 shallots, finely chopped
5 kaffir lime leaves
3 tbsp fish sauce
1 tsp brown sugar
2 tbsp lime juice
2 tsp tamarind paste
6 red or green birdseye chillies, deseeded and pounded
chopped coriander leaves and a few shreds
from a large chilli, to garnish

PREPARATION

1 Small scallops can be used whole, but if you have the larger kind, cut the white meat in half or thirds horizontally. Detach and reserve the corals.
2 Bring a cupful of the coconut milk almost to the boil. Add the lemon grass, shallots and kaffir lime leaves.
3 Stir in the fish sauce, sugar, lime juice and tamarind paste, making sure that the latter dissolves in the liquid. Add the birdseye chillies.
4 Pour in the remaining coconut milk. When hot, put in the white scallop meat and simmer for 3–4 minutes until almost cooked. Add the corals, simmer for one minute more, then remove from the heat. Discard the kaffir lime leaves and serve garnished with the coriander and chilli shreds.

ELIZABETH RAPER'S HERB SOUP

This recipe is based on one in Miss Raper's receipt book, written 1756–1770. During this time she married Dr William Grant, an ancestor of Duncan Grant, the painter. Her receipt book remained in the family and was published in 1924. Serves 6.

INGREDIENTS

2–3 handfuls of sorrel leaves
2–3 handfuls of chervil
handful of beetroot leaves
2 handfuls of parsley leaves
3–4 young leeks or spring onions
¼ green cabbage
1 lettuce
handful of spinach leaves
125g (4oz) butter
1 litre (1¾ pints) good beef stock
4–6 thin slices bread, crusts removed
salt and black pepper

PREPARATION

1 Chop all the herbs and vegetables very finely. Melt the butter in a large saucepan and sauté them for 3–4 minutes.
2 Pour in the stock, add the slices of bread and season with salt and pepper. Bring the soup gently to the boil, then leave to simmer for about 15 minutes or until the bread disintegrates and thickens the soup.

VARIATIONS

Miss Raper notes that peas may be added at the same time as the stock and bread and that, if you want to make a meatless version, the amount of butter should be increased by half and the beef stock replaced by water.

CUCUMBER SOUP WITH BORAGE

A simple chilled summer soup. The borage and cucumber complement each other to give it a delicate yet sustained flavour. If you like buttermilk, try it instead of yogurt, and crème fraîche can replace the thick cream.

INGREDIENTS

2 cucumbers, peeled, deseeded and chopped
5 spring onions, chopped
large handful of borage leaves
300ml (½ pint) cold chicken stock or consommé
300ml (½ pint) natural yogurt
150ml (¼ pint) thick cream
salt and black pepper
pinch cayenne
a few drops lemon juice, optional
borage flowers to garnish, optional

PREPARATION

1 Using a blender or food processor, whizz together the cucumbers, spring onions and most of the borage leaves to make a purée. Add a ladleful or two of the stock to thin the mixture and blend again.

2 Transfer the purée to a large serving bowl or soup tureen.

3 Whisk together the rest of the stock with the yogurt and cream and stir into the cucumber purée. Season with salt, pepper and cayenne and, if you want a sharper flavour, a little lemon juice. Put in the refrigerator and chill thoroughly.

4 Before serving, shred the rest of the borage leaves and scatter them over the soup. If you have any borage flowers, they look very pretty floating on the surface.

PARSLEY SOUP

This vivid green soup has a fine parsley flavour. It can be eaten hot or cold. Serves 6.

INGREDIENTS

2 very large bunches flat-leaf parsley
1 tbsp virgin olive oil
6 spring onions or 4 Welsh onions, thinly sliced
2 cloves garlic, chopped
900ml (1½ pints) vegetable or chicken stock
1 large potato, thinly sliced
salt and black pepper
300ml (½ pint) thick cream or natural yogurt
lemon zest and chopped parsley or mint,
to garnish

PREPARATION

1 Strip the leaves from the parsley. Heat the oil and cook the spring onions, garlic and parsley stalks slowly for about 15 minutes, until soft.
2 Add the stock, potato and seasoning and simmer for about 20 minutes until the potato is soft enough to be crushed with the back of a spoon.
3 Meanwhile, bring a large pan of water to the boil. Add the parsley and, as soon as the water returns to the boil, drain and refresh it under cold water to retain the bright green colour.
4 Purée the parsley leaves and soup base in a food processor or blender, then pass through a sieve. Check the seasoning.
5 If the soup is to be served hot, stir in the cream and reheat gently. To serve chilled, allow to cool completely then stir in the cream. Garnish with lemon zest and parsley or mint.

LOVAGE SOUP

This recipe is from Bohemia and is based on a recipe given to me by Zdena Lancellotti, wife of Angelo Lancellotti, whose salad recipes appear on page 113. Serves 6.

INGREDIENTS

3 medium potatoes, diced
1½ litres (2½ pints) water
salt
2 onions, chopped
2 tbsp sunflower oil or butter
2 tbsp paprika
handful of lovage leaves, chopped
1 egg
2–3 tbsp semolina
salt and black pepper

PREPARATION

1 Put the potatoes to cook in the water with a little salt and bring to a gentle boil. Meanwhile, sauté the onions in the oil until golden. Add the paprika and stir well.
2 Once the paprika has darkened, add the onion mixture to the potato pan. Then add most of the lovage. When the potatoes are cooked, blend and return the soup to the pan. Check the seasoning.
3 Break the egg into a bowl, whisk lightly and add enough semolina to make a firm paste, rubbing the two together as if you were making pastry. Roll it between your fingers into tiny balls or batons and when all are ready drop them into the soup.
4 Gently heat the soup through for 5–10 minutes, then serve, garnished with the remaining lovage.

CHERVIL SOUP

Chervil's light green, lacy leaves produce a pale, delicately coloured soup, which is popular in many north European countries. If you cannot buy big bunches of chervil, it is easy to grow in the garden. Serves 4–6.

INGREDIENTS

60g (2oz) butter
2 shallots, chopped
2 tbsp plain flour
1 litre (1¾ pints) chicken or vegetable stock
2 egg yolks
6 tbsp cream
100g (3½oz) chervil leaves and thin stalks,
finely chopped
salt and black pepper

PREPARATION

1 Melt the butter in a saucepan and soften the shallots for a minute or two, then stir in the flour to form a roux. Keep stirring and cook for a further 3–4 minutes without letting it brown.
2 Warm the stock and add it gradually, stirring constantly, until the mixture is smooth and starts to thicken. Simmer for 20 minutes, stirring from time to time.
3 Beat the egg yolks and mix in the cream and chervil, reserving a little chervil for a garnish.
4 Stir a ladleful of warm soup into the egg and chervil mixture and then pour this all into the pan. Stir well.
5 Heat the soup without letting it boil or it will curdle. Season with salt and pepper and serve at once, scattering a little chervil over each bowl.

PANZANELLA

This peasant dish from Tuscany is currently enjoying a vogue in Italian restaurants. Its success depends on using good quality bread and the best olive oil. Do not be tempted to use factory bread — it won't work.

INGREDIENTS

4 thick slices stale country bread, such as
pane toscano
4 ripe tomatoes
1 red onion, thinly sliced
1 cucumber, deseeded and cubed
handful of basil, using a mixture of green and purple leaves if possible
leaves from a sprig of mint
handful of parsley leaves, preferably flat-leaf
2—3 tbsp red wine vinegar
6—8 tbsp virgin olive oil
salt and black pepper

PREPARATION

1 Cut off and discard the crusts from the bread and leave it to soak in cold water for about 10 minutes. Squeeze the bread dry, then tear it into bite-sized pieces.
2 Core and slice the tomatoes, taking care to reserve any juice that runs from them as you do so.
3 Put the bread into a salad bowl with the tomatoes, including their juice, and the onion and cucumber. Tear the basil leaves into small pieces and chop the mint and parsley roughly. Add them to the bread and vegetables.
4 Whisk together the vinegar and oil to make a dressing and season with salt and pepper.
5 Turn the salad in the dressing, mixing it well so that all the pieces of bread are coated with the oil and vinegar. Check the seasoning.
6 Leave for an hour or so before serving so that the flavours blend.

CEVICHE OF SCALLOPS

*Ceviche comes originally from Peru, where it is usually
served accompanied by thick slices of boiled
sweet potato and corn. Any firm-fleshed fish can be
prepared in this way; the lime or lemon juice marinade
"cooks" the fish. Coriander is the herb used in
South America, but dill is also very good with
delicately flavoured seafood such as scallops.
Serves 4—6.*

INGREDIENTS

*750g (1½lb) scallops
juice of 5—6 limes or lemons
2—3 green chillies, deseeded and finely sliced
3 large tomatoes, skinned, deseeded and diced
1 small red onion, finely chopped
6 tbsp chopped dill
90ml (3 fl oz) olive oil
salt
1 avocado (plus a little lime or lemon juice) and some
sprigs of dill, to garnish*

PREPARATION

1 If you are using large scallops, slice them
through horizontally and detach the corals, but
leave small queen or bay scallops whole.
2 Put them into a dish and add enough lime juice
to cover. Turn the scallops so that all sides are well
coated with juice and cover the dish with clingfilm
or a plate. Leave to marinate in the refrigerator for
3—4 hours. The lime juice brings about a chemical
change similar to that produced by heat, and the
scallops will become opaque.
3 Drain and discard the juice from the scallops
and combine them with the chillies, tomatoes,
onion, chopped dill and olive oil. Season with
a little salt.
4 Return the dish to the refrigerator until ready
to serve. Then peel and slice the avocado, painting
it with lime juice to prevent it from discolouring,
and use it to garnish the scallops along with the
sprigs of dill.

VARIATIONS

Seville orange juice or a mixture of sweet orange
juice and lemon juice can be used as an alternative
marinade. Try it with a mixture of salmon and one
of the white fish such as brill, monkfish, sea bass
or halibut.

Cut the fish into 1—2cm (½—¾in) cubes and
remove any bones. For 750g (1½lb) fish you will
need the juice of 4—5 Seville oranges, or combine
the juice of one sweet orange with that of 4—5
lemons or limes. Replace the dill with coriander.

Red
onion

Tomatoes

Green
chillies

Lime juice

Scallops

Dill

Olive oil

Salt

Avocado

SASHA'S GUACAMOLE

This Mexican dish can be served as a side dish or dip, to accompany tacos, or as a sauce for grilled fish.

INGREDIENTS

5 ripe but firm tomatoes, deseeded and finely cubed
1½ medium onions, finely chopped
4 tbsp finely chopped coriander
2–3 tsp deseeded, chopped jalapeño chilli
salt and black pepper
juice of 1 lime or, if not available, lemon
2 ripe avocados

PREPARATION

1 Put the tomatoes, onions, coriander and chilli into a serving bowl, season to taste with salt and pepper and mix in the lime juice. Cover and refrigerate for 30 minutes to give time for the flavours to blend. Up to this point the guacamole can be made several hours in advance.
2 At the last moment, peel and mash the avocados and stir into the mixture. Serve with corn chips.

BAKED EGGS WITH SORREL

INGREDIENTS

100g (3½oz) sorrel leaves
knob of butter, plus extra for greasing
1 or 2 eggs per person
8 tbsp double cream
black pepper

PREPARATION

1 Heat the oven to 180°C/350°F/gas mark 4. Place a shallow pan of water (bain-marie) inside to warm through.
2 Roll up and shred the sorrel leaves. Cook them in the butter until they have melted into a purée.
3 Generously butter four ovenproof ramekins. Put a layer of sorrel in the bottom of each, then add a tablespoon of cream. Break in one or two eggs and pour over a second tablespoon of cream.
4 Stand the ramekins in the bain-marie and bake for 8–10 minutes, until the eggs are cooked to your liking. Season with black pepper and serve with bread or toast.

MINT AND PARSLEY FRITTATA

Italian frittate are quite thick, unlike French omelettes, and can be served cut into wedges. They are good eaten hot or at room temperature. Serves 4–6.

INGREDIENTS

8 eggs
salt and black pepper
60g (2oz) pecorino cheese, grated
1½ tbsp fresh breadcrumbs
2 tbsp chopped mint
30g (1oz) chopped flat-leaf parsley
2–3 tbsp olive oil

PREPARATION

1 Beat the eggs, season with salt and pepper and mix in the cheese, breadcrumbs and herbs.
2 Heat the oil in a large frying pan and add the egg mixture. Tilt the pan and lift the sides of the frittata as it cooks, so that the runny centre is distributed around the edge of the pan.
3 When the frittata is almost set, and looks golden brown underneath as you lift the edge, turn it over to cook the top for 2–3 minutes. The easiest way is to invert a plate over the pan, tip out the frittata and then slide it back in. Alternatively, put the pan under a preheated grill for a couple of minutes to set the top.

CHIVE FLOWER OMELETTE

This recipe is based on one from the Shaker village of North Union in Ohio, published in The Best of Shaker Cooking *by Amy Bess Miller and Persis Fuller (1970). Serves 2.*

INGREDIENTS

4 large eggs
1 tbsp chopped parsley
1 tbsp chopped chives
1 tbsp chopped chervil
1 tsp chopped tarragon
salt and black pepper
30g (1oz) butter
handful of chive flowers

PREPARATION

1 Beat the eggs lightly, just enough to blend the whites and yolks. Stir in the chopped herb leaves and season with salt and pepper.
2 Heat a heavy frying pan and, when very hot, add the butter. Swirl it around so that the melted butter covers the base and sides. Pour in the egg mixture, shake vigorously and stir with a fork, lifting the mixture at the edges of the pan so that it cooks evenly. This takes only a minute.
3 Scatter the chive flowers over half the omelette, fold it over and slide on to a warm serving dish.

LATKES WITH SALMON

An attractive dish for a first course or for a light meal accompanied by a salad.

INGREDIENTS

375g (12oz) salmon fillet
1 bunch chives or 5–6 small spring onions
2 eggs
4 tbsp plain flour
2 tbsp chopped basil, preferably lemon basil
2 tbsp chopped bergamot leaves
salt and black pepper
3 large potatoes, each weighing about 200g (7oz)
sunflower or light vegetable oil, for frying
Herb Sauce
½ cucumber, deseeded, grated and the liquid squeezed out
100ml (3½fl oz) crème fraîche
4 tbsp mixed chopped herbs, such as parsley, basil, bergamot, anise hyssop or marjoram

PREPARATION

1 If you have a thick salmon fillet cut it lengthwise to give pieces about 1cm (½in) thick, then cut those to make 16 pieces.
2 Chop the chives into 2cm (¾in) lengths. If using spring onions, cut them in half lengthwise first.
3 Whisk the eggs lightly, mix with the flour and herbs and season with salt and pepper. Peel and grate the potatoes and combine them with the egg mixture quickly so they do not turn brown.
4 Heat a few tablespoons of oil in a frying pan, put in 1 tablespoon of the potato mixture, flatten it with the back of a wooden spoon and fry for 1½ minutes. Put a piece of salmon on top, press firmly so that it adheres and cook for another 30 seconds.
5 Turn once and cook for up to 1 minute, until slightly coloured. Drain well on kitchen paper and keep warm. You can fry 2–3 latkes at a time.
6 To make the sauce, stir the cucumber into the crème fraîche and add the herbs. Serve the latkes with the sauce on the side.

HERB PANCAKES WITH SMOKED TROUT

Illustrated overleaf. Serves 6.

INGREDIENTS

100g (3½oz) plain flour
pinch salt
1 egg
1 egg yolk
250ml (8fl oz) milk, or milk and water, preferably carbonated
3–4 tbsp sunflower oil
4–5 tbsp coarsely chopped mixed herbs, such as chervil, parsley, dill or anise, salad burnet, a little young angelica, a little fenugreek, caraway, lemon verbena
6 smoked trout fillets
Horseradish Sauce
125g (4oz) cream cheese or ricotta
100ml (3½fl oz) soured cream
1 tsp grated horseradish, or to taste

PREPARATION

1 Sift the flour with the salt. Whisk the eggs with the milk, add 1 tablespoon of the oil, then whisk in the flour. Beat until smooth – the mixture should have the consistency of a thin cream, so add a little more milk or water if necessary. Strain and add the herbs. Leave to rest for at least 30 minutes.
2 Make the sauce by mixing the cream cheese, soured cream and horseradish. Cover and chill.
3 Remove any bones in the trout using tweezers.
4 To make the pancakes, heat an 18cm (7in) frying pan (preferably non-stick) and brush it lightly with oil. Ladle in a little batter and quickly tilt the pan to spread it evenly over the bottom. When the pancake begins to curl, flick it over with a palette knife, or toss it. The second side takes much less time. Slide it out on to kitchen paper and cover with another sheet. Brush the pan with oil again and make the next pancake. Stack them as you go.
5 To serve, place a trout fillet on each pancake, fold in half and serve the sauce separately.

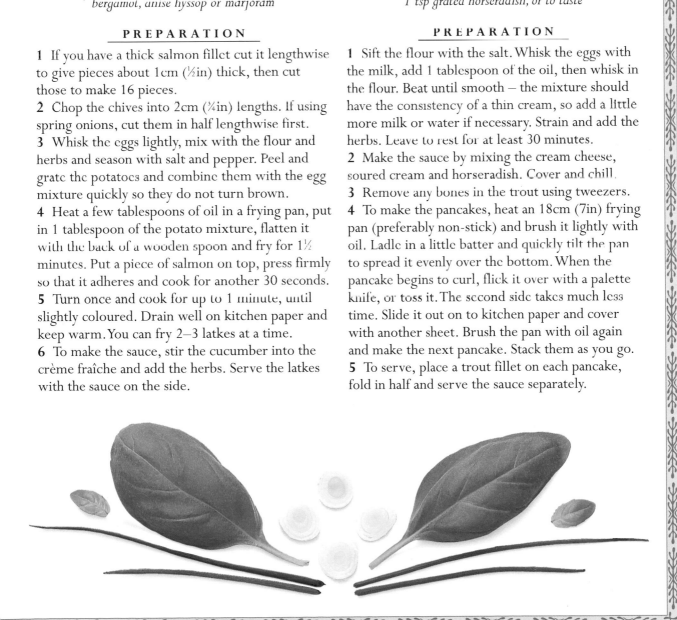

*Herb Pancakes
with Smoked Trout
(see previous page)*

*Moroccan Fish
Tagine with
Chermoula
(see overleaf)*

FISH AND SEAFOOD

Herbs can be used when poaching fish, in marinades and stuffings, and in many sauces used for cooking or served as an accompaniment. Many classic French sauces are flavoured with herbs and make excellent partners for poached and grilled fish.

MOROCCAN FISH TAGINE WITH CHERMOULA

A tagine is a round, flat earthenware dish with a conical lid, and tagine is also the generic word for stews in Morocco. The preserved lemons give a salty sharpness to slow-cooked foods and also to salads. Illustrated on previous page. Serves 6.

INGREDIENTS

1 large or 2 medium sea bass, bream or red snapper, weighing approximately 1.5kg (3lb), scaled and gutted
1 tbsp olive oil
2 cloves garlic, sliced
¼ tsp chilli powder
¼ tsp ground ginger
½ tsp paprika
2 x 400g (13oz) cans chopped tomatoes, drained
salt
handful of green olives
Chermoula
3 cloves garlic, finely chopped
peel from a preserved lemon, chopped (see right)
large bunch flat-leaf parsley, chopped
large bunch coriander, chopped
2 bay leaves
a few sprigs of thyme
1 tsp paprika
½ tsp ground cumin
¼ tsp chilli powder, preferably Moroccan
juice of 1 lemon
6 tbsp olive oil

PREPARATION

1 First make the chermoula by combining all the ingredients to form a thick paste.
2 Slash the sides of the fish in a couple of places to help the heat penetrate evenly. Put it in a tagine or other ovenproof dish and rub well with chermoula, making sure there is some in the cavity and in the cuts. Spread the remaining chermoula under and over the fish. Leave, preferably for several hours, to allow the flavours to develop.
3 Heat the oil and lightly fry the garlic and spices. Add the tomatoes, sprinkle with salt and simmer until the mixture has reduced and thickened somewhat. There must be enough to cover the fish.
4 Heat the oven to 200°C/400°F/gas mark 6.
5 Pour the tomato sauce over the fish. Scatter the olives on top, cover the dish and bake for 40 minutes to 1 hour, depending on the size and number of fish.
6 Traditionally, the fish is served straight from the tagine. Alternatively, arrange it with the sauce on a serving platter. Accompany with rice if you wish.

To make Moroccan preserved lemons, take 4–5 lemons, wash well and cut in four but not all the way through. Sprinkle coarse salt into the cuts, close up the lemons and put them in a large jar. Press down, put a weight on top and close the jar. In a few days sufficient juices should be released to cover the lemons. If not, add more lemon juice. Leave for a month before using and use only the skin, discarding the flesh.

ORIENTAL SKATE SALAD

A quickly assembled first course or light meal.

INGREDIENTS

2 skate wings, weighing approximately 1kg (2lb)
1½ litres (2½ pints) court-bouillon (see right)
1 bunch rocket or watercress, large stalks removed
100g (3½oz) purslane or corn salad
½ red pepper, cut in strips
1 yellow courgette, cut in strips
½ cucumber, cut in strips
4 spring onions, sliced in long, thin strips
½ tsp chopped fresh ginger
½ tsp nigella seed (also known as kalonji)
juice of 1 lime
2 tsp chilli oil, or chilli flakes to taste
3 tbsp sunflower oil
1–2 tsp fish sauce
1–2 tsp light soy sauce
1 tbsp chopped coriander
1 tbsp chopped sweet cicely

PREPARATION

1 Poach the skate wings for 12–15 minutes in the court-bouillon. Strain and leave to cool, then lift the flesh from the bones in long strips.
2 Make a bed of salad herb leaves and arrange the vegetable strips and skate on top.
3 Mix together the ginger, nigella seed, lime juice, oils, fish sauce and soy sauce to make a dressing.
4 Spoon the dressing over the salad, strew the coriander and sweet cicely on top and serve.

To make court-bouillon, bring to the boil 1½ litres water, 1 small glass dry white wine, 2 quartered shallots, 1 sliced carrot, 1 slice lemon, 8 crushed black peppercorns, 1–2 tablespoons herbs (chosen from celery, dill, lovage, marjoram, parsley, savory, tarragon, thyme). Simmer for 30 minutes, strain and use. Court-bouillon can be frozen.

VARIATION

Other salad herbs may be used: balm, burnet, orache and perilla would make good additions.

TUNA WITH SALSA CRUDA

Salsa cruda is a good summer sauce for fried or grilled fish, or for pasta, but it is only worth making if you have ripe, well-flavoured tomatoes.

INGREDIENTS

4 tuna steaks
2 tbsp olive oil, for frying
Marinade
2 bay leaves, crumbled
a few parsley stalks
a few sprigs lemon balm or lemon thyme
salt and black pepper
2 tbsp olive oil
2 tbsp red wine vinegar
Salsa Cruda
500g (1lb) ripe tomatoes, skinned and diced
large handful of basil leaves, chopped
2 cloves garlic, finely chopped
1 red chilli, deseeded and finely chopped
90ml (3fl oz) extra virgin olive oil
salt and black pepper

PREPARATION

1 Put half the herbs for the marinade in a flat dish, just large enough to hold the fish in one layer. Rub the tuna steaks with salt and pepper and add them to the dish. Strew the remaining herbs on top. Pour over the oil and vinegar, cover and leave to marinate for 1–2 hours, turning once.
2 Combine all the ingredients for the salsa cruda an hour or so before serving to allow time for the flavours to blend. Season with salt and pepper and keep at room temperature.
3 Lift the steaks from the marinade and discard the herbs. Heat the oil in a heavy pan and fry the steaks for 3–4 minutes on each side, depending on their thickness. If you prefer to grill or barbecue the steaks, brush them with oil and cook under a preheated grill or over hot coals for about 8–10 minutes, turning once. Serve the salsa cruda in a bowl separately.

VARIATIONS

Other firm fish steaks such as swordfish, salmon or mahi-mahi can be substituted for the tuna.

If you cannot get well-flavoured tomatoes, it would be better to serve the fish with salsa verde, salmoriglio, lovage and lime relish or red pepper relish (for details of how to make them, see pages 138–39). Alternatively, make a quick dressing by blending together a big handful of flat-leaf parsley, 2 shallots, a tablespoon of Dijon mustard, the juice of a lemon and 150ml (¼ pint) olive oil.

BAKED MACKEREL WITH HERBS AND ORANGE SAUCE

This recipe is adapted from William Verral's A Complete System of Cookery, *published in 1759. Buy the fish whole, without having them cleaned, so that the bellies are still intact.*

INGREDIENTS

4 mackerel
small bunch fennel
small bunch salad burnet
small bunch sweet basil
small bunch parsley or chervil
small bunch thyme
a few mint leaves
100g (3½oz) butter, softened
salt and black pepper
glass dry white wine
2 oranges, to garnish
Orange Sauce
2 tbsp chopped shallot or ½ shallot, ½ rocambole
glass dry white wine or fish stock
juice of 2 oranges

PREPARATION

1 Lay the fish on its belly on a work surface and, with a small knife, cut along either side of the backbone to free the two fillets from the bone. Snip the backbone at the head and 2–3cm (1in) above the tail with a pair of scissors, then work it and the ribs free of the flesh, taking care not to pierce the belly. Pull out the backbone (see opposite). Some of the innards may come with it, remove the rest with your finger.
2 Bend back the head to widen the gill openings and take out the gills (see opposite). Wash the fish thoroughly and pat dry.
3 Heat the oven to 200°C/400°F/gas mark 6.
4 Chop all the herb leaves and fine stalks and combine them with the butter. Season with salt and pepper. Divide the herb butter among the cavities of the four fish (see opposite).
5 Arrange the fish side by side in a baking dish, belly-side down, and pour the wine around them. Cover with foil and bake for 15 minutes.
6 Prepare the orange sauce by cooking the shallot in the wine until the liquid has reduced by two-thirds. Add the orange juice and boil a minute or two longer.
7 Cut the two oranges into quarters. To serve, arrange the mackerel, backs uppermost, using the orange quarters to support them, and pour over the hot sauce. A dish of couscous with mixed vegetables makes a good accompaniment.

CLEANING AND STUFFING MACKEREL

1 Holding the fish belly-side down, carefully cut along either side of the backbone. Snip it free at the head and tail. Then work it and the ribs free of the flesh and pull out.

2 Bend back the head of the fish to enable you to put your finger and thumb into the gill opening. Pull out the gills, or cut them out with scissors if necessary, and discard them.

3 Lay the mackerel on its belly and spoon the herb and butter stuffing into the cavity. Keep as neat a shape as possible so that you can easily stand the fish upright in the baking dish.

TEMPURA

*The success of this classic Japanese dish depends
on getting the batter right and on ensuring that the oil
is at the correct temperature for frying each batch of
food, especially the mitsuba and perilla leaves.
Once everything is prepared, it is very quick to
make. Mirin, used in the dipping sauce, is a syrupy,
rice-based wine, used only for cooking. Dashi
is a stock made from dried bonito and kelp. Both
can be found in Japanese stores.*

INGREDIENTS
*flour, for coating
8 large raw prawns
1 medium or large onion
12 stalks mitsuba
4 scallops
4 fresh shiitake or ordinary mushrooms, trimmed
8 perilla leaves
light vegetable oil, for frying*

Dipping Sauce
*4 tbsp mirin or sake
4 tbsp light soy sauce
250ml (8fl oz) dashi
2 tsp grated fresh ginger
3 tbsp grated daikon (mooli) radish*
Batter
*2 egg yolks
500ml (16fl oz) iced water
250g (8oz) plain flour, sifted*

PREPARATION

1 Tempura is best eaten as soon as it leaves the pan
but, if you want to serve everything at the same
time, heat the oven to 180°C/350°F/gas mark 4
to keep the batches warm. Also put ready a bowl of
flour for coating, a draining rack and kitchen paper.
2 Shell the prawns, leaving the tails on. Score
them across the underside 2–3 times and flatten
their backs slightly with the flat blade of a knife
so that they do not curl when fried.

3 Cut the onion across into 4 slices and separate the rings. Alternatively, push 4 toothpicks through the onion, from side to side, and cut between them to give 4 slices. Leave the toothpicks in place.

4 Tie the stalks of mitsuba together in bunches of 3, in a loose knot just below the leaves. Trim the stalks to the same length.

5 Make the dipping sauce by bringing the mirin, soy sauce and dashi to the boil. Remove from the heat and stir in the ginger and radish. Keep warm.

6 Mix half the batter just before starting to fry and do not make the second batch until needed. It should not stand before using. Gently mix an egg yolk with half the water, then tip in half the flour. Stir very lightly with a fork or chopsticks; the mixture should remain lumpy with bits of dry flour in it. If you overmix, it will be heavy.

7 Heat about 6cm (2⅓in) oil in a wok or wide pan to 170–180°C (335–350°F). Test by dropping in a small amount of batter; if it sinks then rises to the surface the temperature is right.

8 Do not crowd the pan; fry a few pieces at a time, according to size. Dip the shellfish and vegetable pieces in the flour, shake off any excess, then coat them in batter and slide them into the oil. Turn frequently with long chopsticks or a slotted spoon. They will need about 3 minutes, until the batter turns a light gold and the pieces rise to the surface.

9 Fry the herbs for about 1 minute. They are not floured. Coat only the stalks, not the leaves, of the mitsuba in batter, and only the underside of the perilla leaves.

10 Drain all the food well and serve with the dipping sauce.

SHRIMPS WITH GREEN SAUCE

This sauce is Mexican, a simpler one than the mole verde on page 68. It is thickened by reduction of the liquid, not by pumpkin seeds, and has less complex flavours.

INGREDIENTS

2 tbsp sunflower or groundnut oil
1kg (2lb) large or medium raw shrimps
Green Sauce
400g (13oz) tomatillos, fresh or canned
3 serrano or jalapeño chillies
4 tbsp chopped coriander leaves
2 tbsp chopped epazote leaves (fresh if possible)
½ tsp ground cumin
2 large lettuce leaves, shredded
½ small onion, chopped
1 clove garlic, chopped
200ml (7fl oz) chicken or vegetable stock
salt

PREPARATION

1 To make the sauce, remove the husks from fresh tomatillos and simmer them in just enough water to cover until soft, about 10 minutes. If canned, drain them. Put with the other sauce ingredients into a blender and process until almost smooth – the mixture should still have some texture.

2 Heat the oil until very hot but not smoking. Add the sauce and fry, stirring constantly, for 3–4 minutes until it thickens and darkens a little.

3 Grill the shrimps for 3–4 minutes until they turn pink, or dry fry them in a heavy non-stick pan over a high heat for about 5 minutes, turning once. Serve with the warm sauce.

FISH BAKED IN A CORIANDER AND NUT SAUCE

This dish of Lebanese origin can be made with any firm white fish such as bream, cod, John Dory, sea bass or snapper.

INGREDIENTS

125g (4oz) walnuts
juice of 1 lemon
good pinch of salt
½ tsp chilli flakes
200g (7oz) coriander leaves
3 cloves garlic
small onion
2 tbsp olive oil
4 fish fillets

PREPARATION

1 Grind the nuts coarsely in a food processor; the sauce should retain a crunchy texture. Add 6 tablespoons water and the lemon juice and blend briefly with the salt and chilli flakes.

2 Heat the oven to 180°C/350°F/gas mark 4.

3 Chop together the coriander, garlic and onion – this can also be done in the food processor. Heat the oil and fry the coriander mixture for a few minutes, then stir in the nuts. Simmer for another 2–3 minutes and check the seasoning.

4 Spread a little of the sauce over the bottom of an ovenproof dish just big enough to take the fillets in a single layer. Place them on the sauce and pour over the remainder.

5 Bake for about 25 minutes, then leave to cool to room temperature before serving.

FISH CURRY

This recipe is from Sri Lanka, but similar versions are found around the coast of southern India and along the Malay peninsula. If you cannot get tamarind paste, use a little lime or lemon juice instead.

INGREDIENTS

2 tbsp mustard or coconut oil
½ tsp fenugreek seeds, lightly crushed
2 onions, sliced
2 cloves garlic, sliced
1 tbsp chopped fresh ginger
½ tsp turmeric
1½ tsp ground cinnamon
1½ tsp ground coriander
2 tsp cumin, dry roasted and ground
3–5 green chillies, deseeded and sliced
1 stalk lemon grass, bottom part only, finely sliced
2 pieces pandanus leaf, 5cm (2in) long
2 sprays curry leaves
1 tbsp tamarind paste
600ml (1 pint) thick coconut milk
salt, optional
750g (1½lb) pomfret, red snapper, sea bass or other firm white fish steaks

PREPARATION

1 Heat the oil in a large heavy pan and quickly sauté the fenugreek seeds until they start to darken. Add the onions and fry them gently until they turn a light gold, about 5–10 minutes. Then add the garlic and ginger and cook, stirring frequently, for a further 2–3 minutes. Do not let them brown.

2 Stir in the spices and herbs – the turmeric, cinnamon, coriander, cumin, chillies, lemon grass, pandanus and curry leaves.

3 Stir the tamarind paste into a few tablespoons of water in a bowl and leave to blend for several minutes, then strain into the pan.

4 Pour in half the coconut milk. (If using creamed coconut, make a thick milk by combining 250g (8oz) with 400ml (14fl oz) water. Put canned coconut milk in the freezer for an hour or two first, so that the thick milk collects at the top. You will need two cans to get sufficient thick milk. The sauce will be too thin if you try to make do with one.) Simmer for 10 minutes, then taste and salt lightly if necessary.

5 Put in the pieces of fish and the rest of the coconut milk. Bring to the boil, then reduce the heat and let the curry simmer for 5–10 minutes, depending on the thickness of the fish. Serve with plain rice garnished with a little fresh coriander.

Coriander

Turmeric

Ginger

Garlic

Onions

Fenugreek

Mustard oil

Pomfret

Cinnamon

Cumin

Green
chillies

Lemon
grass

Pandanus

Curry
leaves

Tamarind
paste

Coconut
milk

Salt

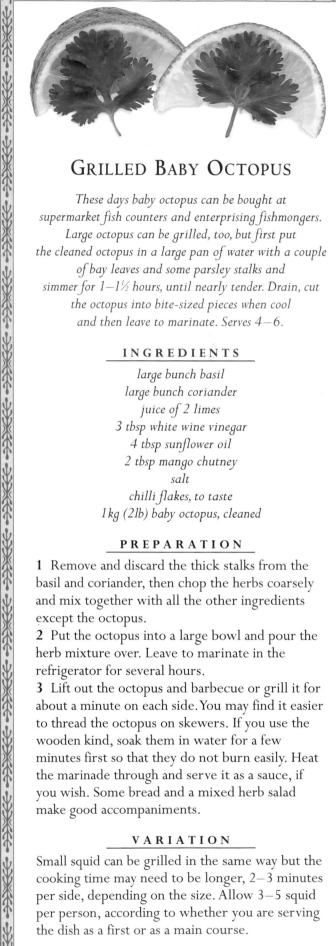

GRILLED BABY OCTOPUS

These days baby octopus can be bought at supermarket fish counters and enterprising fishmongers. Large octopus can be grilled, too, but first put the cleaned octopus in a large pan of water with a couple of bay leaves and some parsley stalks and simmer for 1–1½ hours, until nearly tender. Drain, cut the octopus into bite-sized pieces when cool and then leave to marinate. Serves 4–6.

INGREDIENTS

large bunch basil
large bunch coriander
juice of 2 limes
3 tbsp white wine vinegar
4 tbsp sunflower oil
2 tbsp mango chutney
salt
chilli flakes, to taste
1kg (2lb) baby octopus, cleaned

PREPARATION

1 Remove and discard the thick stalks from the basil and coriander, then chop the herbs coarsely and mix together with all the other ingredients except the octopus.
2 Put the octopus into a large bowl and pour the herb mixture over. Leave to marinate in the refrigerator for several hours.
3 Lift out the octopus and barbecue or grill it for about a minute on each side. You may find it easier to thread the octopus on skewers. If you use the wooden kind, soak them in water for a few minutes first so that they do not burn easily. Heat the marinade through and serve it as a sauce, if you wish. Some bread and a mixed herb salad make good accompaniments.

VARIATION

Small squid can be grilled in the same way but the cooking time may need to be longer, 2–3 minutes per side, depending on the size. Allow 3–5 squid per person, according to whether you are serving the dish as a first or as a main course.

EEL IN GREEN SAUCE

Eel in green sauce is a popular dish throughout Belgium and Holland, but it is made in a slightly different way in the two countries. In Holland, cream and egg yolks are not used and the herbs may be lightly cooked in water before being added to the eel. The Belgian version given here is a richer, more rewarding dish although the flavours of the herbs are less pronounced than in the more austere Dutch version. It can be eaten hot or cold.

INGREDIENTS

1.5kg (3lb) small eels, gutted
90g (3oz) butter
2 shallots, finely chopped
400g (13oz) young spinach, shredded
500g (1lb) sorrel, shredded
large handful of chervil, chopped
large handful of flat-leaf parsley, chopped
a few nettle leaves, chopped (optional)
leaves from 2 sprigs sage, chopped
leaves from 2 sprigs summer or winter savory, chopped
leaves from 2 sprigs thyme, chopped
leaves from 2 sprigs tarragon, chopped
1 large glass dry white wine
salt and black pepper
60ml (2fl oz) thick cream
2 egg yolks, beaten
juice of ½ lemon

PREPARATION

1 Ask the fishmonger to skin the eel or, if this is not possible, take a sharp small knife and loosen the skin around the top of the body. Grasp it firmly and pull downwards toward the tail, holding it in kitchen paper if this gives a better grip. It is quite easy to do but takes confidence.
2 Cut the eels into 5cm (2in) segments, discarding the heads.
3 Heat the butter in a wide pan and gently soften the shallots. Add the eel, sauté for a couple of minutes, then stir in the spinach and herbs. Cover and sweat for 5 minutes.
4 Pour over the wine, season with salt and pepper and cook over a gentle heat until tender, about 10 minutes. If necessary, add more wine or water.
5 Whisk together the cream, egg yolks and some of the lemon juice. Taste, you may need more, depending on the sharpness of the sorrel.
6 Remove the eel using a slotted spoon and keep warm if you are going to serve it hot. Take the pan from the heat and stir in the cream and egg mixture. Heat through very gently for a minute – it must not boil – then pour the sauce over the eel. Serve accompanied by new potatoes or bread.

STUFFED BRILL

This is an elegant dish with a fine flavour. The same stuffing can be used with sole but you would need to allow one fish per person. Serves 2.

INGREDIENTS

1 brill, weighing 750g–1kg (1½–2lb)
2 tbsp dried breadcrumbs
1–2 tbsp olive oil
Stuffing
2 rashers unsmoked streaky bacon, finely chopped
2 mushrooms, finely chopped
3 Welsh onions, tops only, or 2 spring onions, chopped
3–4 Chinese or ordinary chives, chopped
2 tbsp chopped flat-leaf parsley
1 tbsp chopped thyme leaves
1 tbsp chopped summer savory leaves
2 tbsp fresh breadcrumbs
1 egg, lightly beaten
Sauce
2 shallots, finely chopped
1 glass dry white wine
1 tbsp chopped flat-leaf parsley
2 tbsp chopped basil
1 tbsp chopped summer savory leaves
2 tbsp chopped salad burnet
salt and black pepper
100ml (3½fl oz) soured cream

PREPARATION

1 Keep the brill whole but remove the upper dark skin by cutting it across where the tail joins the body. Loosen the skin with the tip of the knife until you can grasp it firmly, then hold the tail down with one hand and pull the skin toward the head with the other.
2 Cut along the backbone with a sharp knife, then lift the flesh of the fillets on either side, cutting out toward the sides. Fold them back and remove the backbone. To do this, bend the fish until the backbone breaks in the middle. Repeat the procedure so that it breaks in 3–4 places and take out the bones.
3 Heat the oven to 180°C/350°F/gas mark 4.
4 Prepare the stuffing by frying the bacon in its own fat, adding a little olive oil if necessary. Add the mushrooms and cook until softened, then put in the Welsh onions and herbs. Mix in enough breadcrumbs to give a medium-firm consistency and bind with most of the egg.
5 Put the brill into a lightly oiled baking dish, and fill the cavity with the stuffing.
6 Draw up the fillets over the stuffing and paint the top of the fish with the remaining beaten egg.

Cover with a light coating of dried breadcrumbs, drizzle olive oil over the top and bake in the oven for about 25 minutes. Shape any leftover stuffing into little patties and fry as an accompaniment.
7 To prepare the sauce, cook the shallots in the wine until the liquid has reduced by two thirds, then add the herbs and season with salt and pepper. Stir in the soured cream, let it just heat through and serve with the fish.

HAKE IN SALSA VERDE

This salsa verde of parsley and garlic comes from the Basque country. The dish is customarily prepared with hake (a much underrated fish outside the Iberian peninsula) but another firm white fish such as haddock or cod could be used. Choose thick fillets cut from a large fish. It is best made in an earthenware casserole that can be put on the top of the stove on a heat diffuser.

INGREDIENTS

750g (1½lb) hake fillets
salt
6 tbsp olive oil
3 cloves garlic, chopped
5 tbsp chopped parsley

PREPARATION

1 Sprinkle the fillets with a little salt. Heat the oil in the casserole over a medium heat and add the garlic. Let it colour gently, taking care that the oil does not get too hot.
2 Add the hake fillets, laying them side by side, scatter with parsley and cover the casserole. Shake frequently as they cook.
3 After 5 minutes remove the lid – the hake will have released some liquid into the dish. Turn the heat to low and continue to cook, uncovered, shaking the dish gently and, if necessary, spooning some of the cooking liquid over the fillets.
4 Cook for a further 5–7 minutes, depending on the thickness of the fish. The sauce should emulsify and thicken during the last minutes of the cooking. Serve from the casserole.

MEAT DISHES

Stews, casseroles and braised meats are inconceivable without herbs; a few sprigs of a single herb, or a bouquet garni, will add depth of flavour to all slow-cooked dishes. Put herbs into marinades and sauces, or throw stalks on the barbecue to add aroma to grills.

PORK FAJITAS IN CHILLI SAUCE WITH SALSA FRESCA

The fajitas have typical Mexican flavourings of chilli and dried herbs — use Mexican or Mediterranean oregano. The moderately pungent dried pasilla chillies could be replaced by other dried varieties — anchos, mulatos or smoky chipotles. In Mexican and south-west American cooking dried chillies are toasted and rehydrated before use.

INGREDIENTS

3 pasilla chillies
1.5kg (3lb) boneless pork loin
½ tsp ground cumin
3 tsp dried oregano
3 tsp dried thyme
juice of 1 lime
juice of ½ orange
½ small onion, sliced
2 cloves garlic
4 tbsp olive oil
Salsa Fresca
4 large ripe tomatoes, skinned, deseeded and chopped
1 red onion, finely chopped
4 pickled or fresh jalapeño chillies
6 tbsp coarsely chopped coriander leaves
juice of 1 lime
2 tbsp tequila
salt

PREPARATION

1 Heat the oven to 240°C/475°F/gas mark 9. Remove the stalks from the chillies and shake out the seeds. Toast them in the oven for 2–3 minutes. Do not let them burn. Transfer them to a bowl, cover with boiling water and soak for 30 minutes.
2 Remove any fat or connective tissue from the meat, then cut it into chunks about 7cm (3in) long. Cut the chunks into flat strips about 2cm (¾in) wide and put them in a glass or china bowl.
3 Put the rest of the ingredients (except those for the salsa) into a food processor. Add the chilli pieces and blend with enough of their soaking liquid to make a marinade that will cover the pork. Pour the marinade over the meat, cover with clingfilm and leave in the refrigerator for 3–4 hours, or longer if you wish.
4 Make the salsa fresca by combining all the ingredients. Cover and refrigerate for at least 30 minutes before serving.
5 Prepare the barbecue or preheat the grill. Take the pork out of the marinade, reserving the latter. Thread the meat on skewers, weaving the skewers in and out along the strips. I find wooden ones the best; if you are going to put them on the barbecue, soak them in water for a few minutes first. Grill over the fire or on a lightly greased tray under a grill for 8–10 minutes, turning once.
6 Heat the marinade to serve as a sauce and accompany with salsa fresca and tortillas or rice.

CHICKEN BREASTS WITH LEMON BALM SALSA

This easily prepared dish is good eaten hot or cold.

INGREDIENTS

4 boneless skinned chicken breasts
3 tbsp lemon juice
4 tbsp olive oil
coarsely ground black pepper
4 tbsp chopped lemon balm leaves
lemon balm sprigs, to garnish
Lemon Balm Salsa
2 tbsp sunflower seeds
1 medium red onion, coarsely chopped
8 sun-dried tomatoes, chopped
3 tbsp chopped lemon balm leaves
salt and black pepper
juice of ½ lemon
1 tbsp lemon balm vinegar (see page 136)
6–8 tbsp (90–120ml) olive oil

PREPARATION

1 Marinate the chicken breasts in the lemon juice, olive oil, black pepper and chopped lemon balm for a few hours in the refrigerator, turning the pieces once.

2 Toss the sunflower seeds in a hot frying pan without oil, dry-roasting them until slightly browned. Grind them coarsely. Mix with all the other ingredients for the salsa. Put it in the refrigerator and allow at least 30 minutes for the flavours to blend before serving.

3 Lift out the meat from the marinade and grill it for about 10 minutes, turning once. Heat the marinade separately in a pan.

4 Arrange the chicken pieces on a serving dish, strain over the cooking liquids and garnish with lemon balm. Serve the salsa separately.

VARIATIONS

Lemon balm salsa makes an excellent partner for other grilled meat and fish dishes.

ORIENTAL CHICKEN AND AUBERGINE PUREE

This recipe is a version of a dish found in Vietnam and Laos, where it is sometimes made with fish or shellfish instead of chicken. The use of lots of herbs and the way of rolling the purée in salad leaves is particularly Vietnamese. Serves 6.

INGREDIENTS

500g (1lb) boneless chicken breasts or thighs, skinned
6 small round oriental aubergines (white, green or purple)
4 tbsp chopped Chinese chives
3 fresh chillies, deseeded and sliced
3 tbsp chopped mint

Dipping Sauce
2 tbsp fish sauce
3 tbsp rice vinegar
1–2 finely sliced chillies
a few shredded mint leaves
pinch or more of sugar, to taste

To Serve
leaves from 1–2 firm-leaf lettuces, such as cos
handful of mint leaves
handful of rao ram or coriander leaves
handful of sweet basil leaves
handful of fine dill sprigs
a few Chinese chives, cut in short lengths

PREPARATION

1 Put the chicken pieces in a pan with enough cold water just to cover and bring to the boil. Lower the heat and simmer for 8–10 minutes, depending on their size. Strain, reserving the liquid. Shred the meat when cool.

2 Heat the oven to 200°C/400°F/gas mark 6. Prick the aubergines in 2–3 places with a fork and bake for about 10 minutes, until soft. Leave to cool, then remove the skins.

3 Combine the ingredients for the dipping sauce and put into small dishes or saucers to serve.

4 Blend the cooked chicken, aubergines, Chinese chives, chillies, mint and 1–2 tablespoons of the poaching liquid in a food processor or pound them to a purée. This should be quite thick, but add a little more liquid if necessary.

5 To serve in the Vietnamese style, arrange the lettuce and herb leaves on platters and put the purée in a bowl. Everyone takes a lettuce leaf, places on it some herb leaves and a spoonful of purée, rolls it up and dips it in the sauce.

PAUPIETTES OF VEAL

Called blinde vinken *in Holland,* Rouladen *in Germany and veal birds in the United States, these small stuffed rolls of veal are popular in many western countries. They can also be made with beef, but then the cooking time must be extended. Serves 6.*

INGREDIENTS

2–3 tbsp sunflower oil
2 shallots, finely chopped
4 cloves garlic, finely chopped
150g (5oz) bacon, chopped
2 thick slices stale firm bread, crusts removed
6 tbsp chopped flat-leaf parsley
2 tsp chopped lemon thyme leaves
2 tsp chopped micromeria or savory leaves
30g (1oz) pine nuts, optional
black pepper
grinding of nutmeg
1 egg
6 veal escalopes, beaten very thin and trimmed (see opposite)
1 glass dry white wine
200ml (7fl oz) veal or chicken stock, or water

PREPARATION

1 Heat 1 tablespoon of the oil in a frying pan and gently fry the shallots, garlic and bacon until all are turning golden.

2 Put the bread through a blender to make coarse crumbs. Tip them into a bowl and add the shallots, garlic and bacon from the pan together with the herbs, pine nuts and meat trimmings. Season well with pepper and nutmeg and stir in the egg to bind the mixture.

3 Spread out the pieces of veal and season lightly if you wish. Put a spoonful of the stuffing at one end of each, then roll up and secure with toothpicks or string (see opposite).

4 Set the oven to 160°C/325°F/gas mark 3.

5 Heat the remaining oil in a pan that will take the paupiettes in one layer and can also go in the oven. Brown them lightly on all sides, then add the wine and simmer for a few minutes more, turning once or twice. Pour in the stock and bring back to the boil.

6 Cover the pan with a lid or foil and transfer to the oven. Cook for about 45–50 minutes, until the meat is tender.

7 Remove the paupiettes to a warm serving platter and boil down the cooking juices to make a sauce. A purée of broad beans flavoured with savory or mint, or some mashed potato, makes a good accompaniment.

PREPARING THE PAUPIETTES

1 Lay the escalopes between two sheets of clingfilm or greaseproof paper, and lightly pound with a mallet or rolling pin until about 3mm (⅛in) thick. Trim the edges to a neat shape.

2 Put a spoonful of herb stuffing at the end of each escalope. Roll it up, not too tightly as the filling will expand a little during cooking, but not so loosely that the stuffing falls out.

3 Secure the rolls with toothpicks, turning in the ends if the pieces of meat are large enough. Alternatively, you can tie them around once or twice with a piece of fine string.

Iranian Lamb and Herb Stew

A richly flavoured stew of beans, lamb, herbs and dried limes. The limes are a speciality of Iran and can be found in Iranian shops, as can powdered dried lime. However, it is easy to dry limes yourself if you leave them on a radiator for several months until they are hard and sound hollow when tapped. Fenugreek is an essential herb for this stew. It is easy to grow in summer, but it can also be bought dried from Iranian and Indian shops.

INGREDIENTS

100g (3½oz) red kidney beans, soaked overnight
4 tbsp sunflower oil
1 large onion, chopped
500g (1lb) lean lamb, cubed
1 tsp turmeric
black pepper and salt
juice of 2 lemons
2–3 leeks, finely chopped
250g (8oz) spinach, chopped
200g (7oz) flat-leaf parsley, chopped
60g (2oz) coriander or celery leaves, chopped
leaves from a few sprigs fresh fenugreek
or 1 tbsp dried leaves
5 dried limes

PREPARATION

1 Strain the beans and cook in fresh unsalted water for 15–20 minutes, then drain them, rinse and set aside.
2 Heat half the oil in a large heavy pan and sauté the onion. Add the lamb and brown it on all sides. Stir in the turmeric and season with pepper and a little salt. Pour over the lemon juice and just enough boiling water to cover the meat. Cover and simmer for 30 minutes.
3 Heat the remaining oil and sauté the leeks, spinach and herbs for 10–15 minutes until they darken. Add this mixture to the meat along with the beans.
4 Pierce the limes in 2–3 places and add them to the pan. Make sure there is enough liquid just to cover all the ingredients and simmer for an hour, checking occasionally that nothing is sticking.
5 Serve with rice. Although they are not eaten, the limes are usually left in the dish.

VARIATION

Black-eyed peas can be used as an alternative to red kidney beans.

Guinea Fowl with Young Garlic and Herbs

Fresh garlic is in the shops in late spring. The dish can be made at other times of the year with dried garlic. As with fresh, separate the cloves and remove the outer papery layers but do not peel them. The delicate flavour of new garlic is particularly suited to guinea fowl; with older garlic a chicken might be a better choice. Illustrated overleaf.

INGREDIENTS

90ml (3fl oz) olive oil
1 guinea fowl, weighing approximately 1.5kg (3lb)
2 heads fresh garlic
2 long sprigs rosemary
6–8 sprigs thyme
2 bay leaves
4 sprigs sage
6–8 stalks parsley
2 sprigs costmary, optional
juice of 1 lemon
salt and black pepper
chopped parsley, to garnish

PREPARATION

1 Heat the oven to 180°C/350°F/gas mark 4.
2 Pour a tablespoon of the oil into a frying pan and brown the guinea fowl lightly on all sides.
3 Split the heads of garlic into cloves. There is no need to peel fresh new garlic, but it is better to snip off the long tapering skins at the tops of the cloves. Pour the rest of the oil into a deep casserole dish, just large enough to hold the bird, and add the garlic.
4 Tie the herbs into three small mixed bundles. (This makes it easier to remove them later.) Put one inside the guinea fowl, then put the bird on top of the garlic with the other two herb bouquets on either side. Pour over the lemon juice and season with salt and pepper.
5 Cover the dish with a double layer of foil as well as the lid to seal it as tightly as possible and cook for 1½ hours.
6 Lift out the guinea fowl and leave it to rest for 10 minutes in a warm place. Discard the herbs and strain the garlic, reserving the pan juices. Pass the garlic through a sieve or mash it with a fork.
7 Pour off as much excess oil as possible, then reheat the pan juices and pour them into a sauce boat to serve. Carve the guinea fowl and arrange on a serving platter. Add the garlic purée and garnish with a little parsley.

JAMBON PERSILLE

This is the traditional Easter dish of Burgundy, marbled pink and green and set in a pale gold jelly. The local charcutiers make it with a whole ham, but it can be made at home using a piece of gammon. Illustrated overleaf. Serves 8–10.

INGREDIENTS

2kg (4lb) piece of gammon
2 carrots, chopped
4 cloves garlic, chopped
2 calf's feet
large bouquet garni made up of bay leaves and sprigs
of thyme, tarragon and flat-leaf parsley
2 onions, each stuck with 1 clove
8 black peppercorns
1 bottle dry white wine
3 shallots
60g (2oz) flat-leaf parsley
3–4 tbsp white wine vinegar

PREPARATION

1 Soak the gammon for 18–24 hours to remove excess salt, changing the water two or three times. Drain and set aside.
2 Put the carrots and garlic in a large pan with the calf's feet, bouquet garni, onions and peppercorns. Place the gammon in the middle, pour over the wine and enough water to cover.
3 Bring to the boil, skim, and lower the heat. Simmer gently for 3–4 hours, adding more water if necessary. Skim the surface from time to time, as needed, to remove fat. When the gammon pierces easily with a fork, remove the pan from the heat and leave to cool slightly. Lift out the ham and calf's feet and discard the latter.
4 Boil down the stock to about 1 litre (1¾ pints) and skim thoroughly. Strain through a sieve lined with a double layer of muslin. Taste and add pepper if necessary – it should be quite highly seasoned.
5 Chop the shallots and parsley and mix together.
6 Pull the ham into large chunks with your fingers or using two forks. Put a layer in the bottom of a large glass or china bowl, then a layer of parsley. Sprinkle over a spoonful of vinegar and ladleful of stock, letting them run down between the pieces of ham. Repeat the layers until the ham and parsley are used up and pour over the remaining stock.
7 Press down the meat, making sure all is below the liquid. Cover with a plate of almost the same diameter, put a weight on top and chill for 12 hours. Serve from the bowl, or turn out, as you wish. Small gherkins are a good accompaniment, and some crusty bread.

PORK AND CRAB SALAD

A fresh tasting salad in which the ingredients can be varied according to what is available: chicken and shrimps may replace the pork and crab, white or red radish may be added. The inspiration for the salad is Vietnamese, so bean sprouts and bamboo shoots in place of the tomato and pepper would make it quite authentic. It is important to have a variety of herbs, but they can be changed to suit your taste. Try lemon or sweet basil, coriander in place of rao ram, anise or anise hyssop for the fennel, catnip or calamint for the mint. Serve as a first course. Illustrated on page 99.

INGREDIENTS

100g (3½oz) piece of pork loin
100g (3½oz) white crab meat, cooked
1 tbsp sesame seeds
1 lettuce
2 plum tomatoes, deseeded and sliced in strips
2 green peppers, preferably the long, pale green type,
deseeded and sliced in strips
½ cucumber, very thinly sliced
3 spring onions, finely sliced
2 carrots, cut in slivers
4 sprigs Thai basil
3–4 sprigs fennel
6 sprigs rao ram
4 sprigs mint
Nuoc Cham Dressing
2 tbsp unsalted peanuts
1 tbsp chilli oil
2 tsp sugar, or to taste
4 tbsp water
4 tbsp fish sauce
5–6 tbsp (75–90ml) lime juice

PREPARATION

1 Put the pork in a pan with just enough cold water to cover. Bring to the boil, reduce the heat and simmer until tender, about 20 minutes. Leave in the water for 10 minutes, then strain and put aside until cold.
2 Shred the crab meat and slice the pork into very thin rounds. Dry-roast the sesame seeds until golden (for method, see page 93).
3 Line a platter with lettuce leaves. Arrange the tomatoes, peppers, cucumber, spring onions, carrots and herb leaves on the lettuce. Top with the pork and crab meat. Scatter over the sesame seeds.
4 Make the nuoc cham dressing by dry-roasting the peanuts until they have darkened a little. Grind them coarsely and mix with all the other dressing ingredients. Stir well then spoon it over and serve.

Jambon Persillé
(see previous page)

Guinea Fowl with
Young Garlic and Herbs
(see page 96)

Pork and Crab Salad
(see page 97)

ARISTA ALLA FIORENTINA
Italian roast pork with rosemary

Illustrated on page 65. Serves 6.

INGREDIENTS

*1kg (2lb) pork loin, boned and with the skin and
most of the fat removed
a few sprigs rosemary
2 cloves garlic, finely chopped
salt and black pepper
a few crushed cloves or juniper berries, optional
2 tbsp olive oil
1 glass dry white wine or water*

PREPARATION

1 Heat the oven to 180°C/350°F/gas mark 4.
2 Cut a deep slit lengthwise down the joint, making sure it does not pierce the other side.
3 Strip the rosemary leaves from the stalks, chop them finely and mix with the garlic. Put some of the mixture into the pocket in the meat and spread the rest over the flesh. Season with salt and pepper.
4 Roll up the meat and tie around with string at regular intervals. Rub the outside of the roll with the crushed cloves and put into a roasting tin, lightly greased with 1 tablespoon of the oil. Pour the remaining oil over the pork.
5 Put the joint into the oven and allow it to brown, turning once or twice. Pour over the wine and continue to cook for an hour or so, basting occasionally, until most of the liquid has evaporated and the meat is cooked through.
6 Leave the joint to rest for 10 minutes before slicing it thinly. Arista is good eaten hot or cold.

LAMB KLEFTIKO
Baked lamb with oregano

This Greek village dish uses thick slices cut from a leg of lamb across the bone, but it also works well with large chops. In Greece it would be made with rigani (dried oregano, see pages 16–17). Parchment paper for wrapping the parcels will look more attractive than foil. Illustrated on page 65.

INGREDIENTS

*4 slices cut from a leg of lamb, about 4cm (1½in) thick
5 tbsp (75ml) olive oil
1 large clove garlic, cut into slivers
salt and black pepper
2 tbsp chopped fresh oregano, or 1 tbsp dried
juice of 1 lemon*

PREPARATION

1 Heat the oven to 200°C/400°F/gas mark 6.
2 Cut 4 pieces of parchment paper or foil, large enough to wrap the pieces of lamb individually, and brush with a tablespoon of oil.
3 Wipe the meat, taking care to remove any splinters of bone, and place each slice in the centre of a piece of parchment or foil. Make some small incisions and stud the meat with slivers of garlic. Season and scatter over the oregano. Sprinkle with lemon juice and the remaining oil.
4 Close the parcels neatly, folding and crimping the edges or tying them, to make sure they cannot leak. Bake in the oven for 10 minutes, then reduce the heat to 180°C/350°F/gas mark 4 and continue to cook for a further 40 minutes.
5 Undo the parcels but leave the wrapping in place to serve.

SALTIMBOCCA ALLA ROMANA
Veal with Parma ham and sage

A quickly cooked dish to serve with puréed or sautéed potatoes or a celeriac purée flavoured with lovage. The scaloppine are made from beaten escalopes, as shown on page 95. The dish is illustrated on page 64.

INGREDIENTS

*4 large thin slices of Parma ham
8 veal scaloppine, about 12cm (5in) square
8 sage leaves
60g (2oz) butter
salt and black pepper
½ glass dry white wine*

PREPARATION

1 Cut the slices of Parma ham in half. Put one piece on top of each scaloppine, trimming it if necessary, then top each with a sage leaf, pinning the layers together with toothpicks.
2 Heat the butter in a frying pan large enough to hold the scaloppine in a single layer. Put in the meat, veal side down, and fry for 2–3 minutes, then turn and cook the other side. Season with salt and pepper.
3 Pour over the wine. When it bubbles, lift out the meat, remove the toothpicks, leaving the sage leaves on top, and keep warm. Scrape any bits from the bottom of the pan, pour the juices over the meat and serve. The whole process should not take more than about 5 minutes.

GRILLED STEAK WITH BEARNAISE SAUCE

Illustrated on page 64.

INGREDIENTS

4 fillet or sirloin steaks
olive oil
salt and black pepper
Béarnaise Sauce
150ml (¼ pint) dry white wine
3 tbsp white wine or tarragon vinegar
3 shallots, finely chopped
5 sprigs tarragon
freshly ground white pepper
175g (6oz) unsalted butter
3 egg yolks
salt
1 tbsp finely chopped tarragon leaves or a mixture of tarragon and chervil

PREPARATION

1 To make the béarnaise sauce, put the white wine, vinegar, shallots, sprigs of tarragon and a good grinding of white pepper into a small heavy pan over a low heat. Simmer, uncovered, for 10–15 minutes, until the liquid has reduced to 2–3 tablespoons.
2 Strain through a fine sieve, pressing the shallots and tarragon well to extract all the flavour. Return the liquid to the pan.
3 Melt the butter gently in a separate small pan and set aside. When it has cooled to lukewarm, pour off the clear liquid to use later, and discard the white residue.
4 Set the pan with the wine and vinegar infusion over a very low heat and whisk in the egg yolks and a little salt. Then add the melted butter, a tablespoon or so at a time, whisking continuously. Do not add more butter until each spoonful has been absorbed. Remove the pan from the heat before adding the final spoonful – it will still be hot enough to go on cooking the sauce.
5 Stir in the finely chopped tarragon and check the seasoning.
6 Prepare the barbecue or preheat the grill. Rub the steaks lightly on both sides with olive oil and season with salt and pepper just before putting them to cook.
7 Sear the meat on both sides, about 1 minute per side. The rest of the grilling time will depend on the thickness of the steaks and how well you like them cooked. For a 5–6cm (2–2½in) thick fillet steak allow a total cooking time, including searing, of 6–8 minutes for rare; 8–10 minutes for medium rare; 10–12 minutes for medium. For a 2½–3cm (1in) thick sirloin steak allow 5–6 minutes for rare; 6–7 for medium rare and 7–9 for medium. It is best not to turn the meat more than once while grilling in order to preserve the juices that collect on the top. Serve with the sauce.

VARIATION

By substituting mint for tarragon in the béarnaise sauce you can make *sauce paloise*. Fine and sharply flavoured, this makes an excellent accompaniment for grilled chicken and meat or poached salmon.

PORK NOISETTES WITH FENNEL

Illustrated on pages 64–65.

INGREDIENTS

3–4 tbsp olive oil
10 shallots, finely chopped
2 tsp crushed fennel seeds
salt and black pepper
8 pork noisettes
1 bunch fennel
2 bay leaves
1 glass Calvados

PREPARATION

1 Lightly oil an ovenproof dish large enough to take the noisettes in a single layer. Make a bed of shallots and fennel seeds in the bottom, season lightly with salt and pepper and put the meat on top. Season again.
2 Cut most of the fennel leaves from the stalks. Keep back the leaves, but strew the stalks and bay leaves around and over the meat. Dribble a little olive oil over the surface. If you can, prepare the dish to this point a few hours before you want to cook it so that the meat has time to start absorbing the flavours of the herbs.
3 Heat the grill and set the oven to 150°C/300°F/gas mark 2.
4 Put the dish under the grill for 2–4 minutes, depending on the thickness of the noisettes, so that they colour slightly. Pour over the Calvados, cover tightly with foil and put the dish into the oven to cook slowly for 45–50 minutes. Check after 20 minutes and turn the noisettes.
5 Chop the fennel leaves finely. Before serving, remove the fennel stalks and bay leaves. Scatter the fennel leaves over the meat and serve straight from the dish. The noisettes are excellent eaten with mashed sweet potato, flavoured with a little sherry and chopped parsley, and a green salad.

VEGETABLE DISHES

Herbs are most often added to vegetables as a last minute garnish, but they can play a more substantial role. Provençal vegetable dishes are always aromatic with herbs; the Turks excel in flavouring vegetable dishes with combinations of dill, mint and parsley.

TIAN OF TOMATOES AND PEPPERS

A tian is a shallow earthenware dish from Provence that has given its name to the vegetable dishes cooked in it. Serves 6.

INGREDIENTS

4 red peppers
6 large tomatoes
10 anchovy fillets
large handful of basil leaves
1 tbsp chopped thyme leaves
½ tbsp chopped winter savory leaves
3 cloves garlic, chopped
75g (2½oz) small black olives
black pepper
4–5 tbsp freshly made breadcrumbs
3–4 tbsp olive oil

PREPARATION

1 Put the peppers under a grill or directly on to a gas flame, turning them frequently until they are charred on all sides. Leave to cool in a plastic bag, then strip off the skin under cold running water. Halve them and remove stalks and seeds. Dry on kitchen paper and cut into slices.
2 Heat the oven to 200°C/400°F/gas mark 6.
3 Immerse the tomatoes in boiling water for a few seconds. Drain and skin them and cut into thick slices. Cut the anchovy fillets in half and tear the basil leaves into small pieces.
4 Lightly oil a tian or other gratin dish and line the bottom with a layer of tomatoes (about a third). Spread over them half the anchovies, a sprinkling of herbs and garlic and half the olives. Season with black pepper. Cover with a layer of half the peppers, followed by another layer of tomatoes. Repeat the anchovies, herbs, garlic, olives and black pepper seasoning. Add the rest of the peppers and a final layer of tomatoes.
5 Scatter the breadcrumbs on top, drizzle over the oil and bake for 30 minutes. Serve warm or cold, but not chilled.

Winter savory

Thyme

Basil

Anchovy fillets

Red peppers   *Tomatoes*

Garlic

Black olives

Black pepper

Fresh breadcrumbs

Olive oil

BROAD BEANS IN OLIVE OIL

In this Turkish-inspired dish, the water evaporates during the slow cooking, leaving a rich sauce that is not at all greasy. Shelled older beans can be used, but you will need to increase the quantity.

INGREDIENTS

1kg (2lb) fresh young broad beans, in their pods
salt
juice of ½ lemon
2 bunches spring onions, cut into short lengths
4 tbsp chopped summer savory
6 tbsp chopped dill or anise hyssop
2 tsp sugar
100ml (3½fl oz) olive oil
200ml (7fl oz) water
yogurt and garlic, to serve (optional)

PREPARATION

1 Top, tail and string the beanpods, cutting the larger ones in half. Sprinkle them with salt and pour over the lemon juice.
2 Put about a third of the beans, including all the larger ones, in the bottom of a heavy pan and spread half the spring onions and half the herbs over them. Add another layer of beans, the rest of the spring onions and herbs, then top with the last of the beans.
3 Sprinkle over the sugar, and add the olive oil and water. Cover the pan with a sheet of moistened greaseproof paper and a tight-fitting lid. Cook over a moderate heat for about an hour, shaking the pan occasionally to prevent sticking. The beans should be tender but still whole.
4 Remove from the heat and leave to cool in the pan. Turn the beans into a serving dish and serve cool or cold. If you wish, accompany them with a bowl of yogurt flavoured with crushed garlic.

JERUSALEM ARTICHOKES WITH PIEDS DE MOUTON

Pieds de mouton mushrooms have a particular affinity with Jerusalem artichokes, just as chanterelles have with Chinese artichokes (crosnes). Here are two recipes in one, the difference being in the preparation of the artichokes.

INGREDIENTS

500g (1lb) Jerusalem artichokes
juice of ½ lemon
60g (2oz) butter
500g (1lb) pieds de mouton
3 shallots, finely chopped
1 tbsp chopped thyme
1 tbsp chopped marjoram
2 tbsp chopped flat-leaf parsley
salt and black pepper
small glass dry white wine or sherry
2–3 tbsp cream, optional

PREPARATION

1 Peel the artichokes, cut into pieces and drop into water and lemon juice. Blanch them for 2–3 minutes in fresh boiling water and drain. Melt half the butter and sauté them until almost tender.
2 Wipe the mushrooms and cut into similar-sized pieces. Heat the rest of the butter and sauté the shallots until soft, turn up the heat and add the mushrooms. Sauté briskly for 2–3 minutes, then add the artichokes and herbs and season well.
3 Pour over the wine, cover and simmer for about 5 minutes. Remove the vegetables to a serving dish. If necessary, boil down the cooking liquor, and stir in a little cream, to taste.

VARIATION

For an even more delicate dish, top and tail Chinese artichokes. Simmer for 5 minutes in enough water to cover plus a little butter. Drain, reserving the liquid. Cook the shallots and chanterelles as above, add the herbs and artichokes with a little cooking liquid instead of wine and simmer 3–4 minutes.

STUFFED CABBAGE WITH HYSSOP

A hearty dish to serve as a main course with good bread or potatoes. Serves 6.

INGREDIENTS

*1 large green cabbage
100g (3½oz) rice
2 tbsp olive oil
1 large onion, finely chopped
3 cloves garlic, finely chopped
150g (5oz) piece of streaky bacon or spek (a north European speciality bacon), cubed
2 large tomatoes, skinned, deseeded and chopped
100g (3½oz) peas
250g (8oz) sausage meat or minced pork
2 tbsp chopped hyssop leaves
salt and black pepper
approximately 750ml (1¼ pints) chicken or vegetable stock
sprigs of hyssop, to garnish*

PREPARATION

1 Trim away the outermost leaves from the cabbage and cut off the stalk. Blanch the cabbage for 5 minutes in boiling water. Refresh it with cold water and drain well. Carefully separate the leaves. Cut out the lower part of the central rib of the biggest leaves.
2 Parboil the rice for 10 minutes, refresh under cold running water and drain thoroughly.
3 Heat the oil, lightly sauté the onion until it is pale in colour, add the garlic and bacon and cook gently for 2–3 minutes more.
4 Chop the inner small leaves of the cabbage. Put the onion and bacon mixture into a large bowl and add the other ingredients for the stuffing: the chopped cabbage leaves, rice, tomatoes, peas, sausage meat and hyssop. Season well and mix together thoroughly.
5 Heat the oven to 180°C/350°F/gas mark 4.
6 Line a bowl with a net or piece of muslin and spread over it the large leaves, to reconstitute the cabbage. Put the stuffing in the centre and fold the leaves over it to form a ball. Tie up the net or muslin to keep it in shape.
7 Transfer the cabbage to an ovenproof casserole, add enough stock to fill it by two thirds, cover tightly and bake in the oven for 2 hours.
8 To serve, lift out the cabbage with a slotted spoon, remove the muslin and put the cabbage into a large bowl. Keep it warm while you boil the cooking liquor to reduce it by half. Garnish with a few hyssop sprigs and serve the sauce separately.

BUTTERNUT SQUASH WITH TARRAGON

Serves 2–3.

INGREDIENTS

*1 butternut squash, weighing approximately 500g (1lb)
60g (2oz) butter
black pepper
1½ tbsp chopped fresh tarragon or 2 tsp crumbled dried*

PREPARATION

1 Peel and halve the squash, remove the seeds and fibrous parts and cube the flesh. Melt the butter in a pan and cook the squash gently, covered, for 10–15 minutes. Alternatively, cook the unpeeled squash halves in a microwave oven. Put the butter into the cavities, cover with microwave clingfilm and cook for 10 minutes.
2 Purée the squash, season with pepper, and stir in the tarragon. If necessary, add more butter. It is good served with pork noisettes (see page 101).

LENTILS FLAVOURED WITH ORIENTAL HERBS

The use of oil or butter, aromatized with herbs or spices, to finish a dish of lentils is basic to Indian cooking. Vary the herbs to your taste, but use enough; lentils can absorb a lot of flavouring.

INGREDIENTS

*250g (8oz) small, dark green Puy lentils
2 bay leaves
1 medium onion, whole
6 tbsp sunflower or olive oil
2–3 tbsp chopped coriander
1 tbsp chopped coriander root
2–3 tbsp chopped basil, preferably anise or Thai
2 tbsp chopped mint, preferably Tashkent or lemon
salt and black pepper
2 tbsp chopped holy basil*

PREPARATION

1 Cook the lentils in unsalted water with the bay leaves and onion until tender, about 25 minutes. Drain thoroughly, discarding the onion and bay.
2 Heat the oil in a large pan and fry all the herbs, except the holy basil, for 3–4 minutes.
3 Stir in the cooked lentils, heat through and season with salt and pepper. Add the holy basil. Serve with rice as part of a vegetarian meal or to accompany meat or fish.

CELERY STAMPPOT

Stamppot is a traditional Dutch winter dish of potato mashed with another vegetable or with apples. Leeks, carrots, kale, cabbage and onions are commonly used; this version uses cutting celery. It is a strong-flavoured herb which in parts of northern Europe is used to some extent as a garnish, as parsley is used elsewhere. I prefer it cooked rather than raw. If you want to try a different herb, select something with a clear flavour such as coriander, savory or lovage.

INGREDIENTS

4 large potatoes
large bunch cutting celery, weighing approximately
100g (3½oz)
125g (4oz) butter
3–4 tbsp thick natural yogurt
black pepper and salt

PREPARATION

1 Boil the potatoes in salted water, then drain.
2 Remove the thick celery stalks and chop the leaves coarsely in a food processor. Sauté briefly in half the butter, then add them to the potatoes and mash, adding more butter as necessary.
3 Add the yogurt. I find this helps bring out the taste of the celery while tempering its bitterness.
4 Season with pepper, and a little salt if necessary. Reheat and serve.

MORELS WITH GARLIC AND HERBS

This is a lovely late spring dish; the fresh morels, mild new garlic and herbs all appear at the same time and the flavours blend beautifully.

INGREDIENTS

500g (1lb) fresh morels
100g (3½oz) butter
3 cloves new garlic, crushed and coarsely chopped
2 tbsp chopped chervil
1 tbsp chopped summer savory
2 tbsp chopped basil or parsley
1 tbsp chopped tarragon

PREPARATION

1 Halve the morels lengthways and wash well, with a little salt in the water. Drain thoroughly and stew them gently in the butter for 10 minutes. Add the garlic and cook for a further 5 minutes.
2 Turn the morels into a serving dish and stir in the mixed herbs. Serve at once.

STUFFED COURGETTE FLOWERS

This Greek dish must be made with freshly picked courgette or pumpkin flowers, before they begin to fade and crumple. In southern Europe the flowers are readily available in season from markets and greengrocers. Further north they are often sold with a small courgette still attached. A little grated courgette can be added to the stuffing if you wish. Serves 6.

INGREDIENTS

2–3 tbsp olive oil
2 cloves garlic, finely chopped
1 bunch spring onions or Welsh onion tops,
finely chopped
200g (7oz) long-grain rice
2 tbsp tomato purée
1 tsp sugar
salt and black pepper
pinch of cinnamon
3 tbsp chopped flat-leaf parsley
1 tbsp chopped mint
2 tbsp chopped fennel
24 courgette flowers
1 egg, beaten
lemon juice, to taste

PREPARATION

1 Heat the oil and sauté the garlic and spring onions until soft. Stir in the rice and tomato purée and season with sugar, salt, pepper and cinnamon. Add the parsley, mint and fennel and make sure that all the ingredients are evenly distributed through the mixture.
2 Fill each flower carefully, folding the tops of the petals over the stuffing (see opposite). Put them into a large frying or other shallow pan in which they will fit in a single layer, cover with water and bring gently to the boil. Reduce the heat and simmer for about 25 minutes, until the rice is cooked. Check occasionally to see if the water needs topping up. Remove from the heat and leave to stand for a few minutes.
3 Lift out the flowers with a slotted spoon. Reduce the cooking liquid a little if necessary: there should be about 250ml (8fl oz). Remove the pan from the heat and whisk in the beaten egg to thicken it further. Add lemon juice to taste, pour over the courgette flowers and serve at room temperature, the Greek way, as a first course or to accompany roast lamb.

STUFFING COURGETTE FLOWERS

1 Gently fold back the petals of the courgette flowers.

2 Spoon in the stuffing, carefully pushing it down to the base. Do not overfill or the flowers may burst when the rice swells during cooking.

3 Fold the tops of the petals over the stuffing. The flowers have a slightly elastic texture that should keep the mixture securely wrapped inside.

NEW POTATOES WITH FENUGREEK

This classic north Indian dish is made with very tiny potatoes. If you cannot get really small ones, use new potatoes cut in half or quartered.

INGREDIENTS

250g (8oz) fresh fenugreek leaves or 2 tbsp dried (see
Iranian Lamb Stew on page 96)
4–5 tbsp sunflower or groundnut oil
1 tsp cumin seeds
1 green chilli, chopped (optional)
½ tsp turmeric
500g (1lb) new potatoes
½ tsp garam masala
salt
1 tbsp lemon juice or more, to taste

PREPARATION

1 Discard any fenugreek stalks, whether using fresh or dried. Wash fresh leaves in several changes of water and chop them. Rinse dried leaves.
2 Heat the oil in a heavy, wide pan and add the cumin seeds. When they change colour, after 20 seconds or so, add the chilli and turmeric, stir and put in the potatoes. Fry for 5 minutes over a medium heat, stirring constantly.
3 Add the fenugreek leaves, lower the heat and cook for a further 4–5 minutes, still stirring, until the greens are wilted. Sprinkle with garam masala and a little salt.
4 Cover the pan tightly and leave on a very low heat for 20–25 minutes, until the potatoes are cooked. Stir gently once or twice. Usually no liquid is added but, if the potatoes become too dry, sprinkle them with a tablespoon or two of water.
5 When the potatoes are cooked, add the lemon juice to taste and serve.

SPINACH AND HERB TART

INGREDIENTS

150g (5oz) spinach
150g (5oz) sorrel
150g (5oz) flat-leaf parsley
150g (5oz) chervil
1 lettuce heart
a few borage leaves
1 bunch spring onions or Welsh onion tops
3 eggs
300ml (½ pint) thick cream
4 tbsp fresh breadcrumbs
salt and black pepper
250g (8oz) filo pastry
60g (2oz) butter, melted

PREPARATION

1 Boil the spinach, sorrel and other herbs in plenty of water for a few minutes. Drain and press to squeeze out all the water, then chop coarsely.
2 Chop the spring onions and stir into the herb mixture. Whisk the eggs lightly. Heat the cream with the breadcrumbs and stir until it thickens slightly. Stir in the eggs and herbs and season.
3 Heat the oven to 180°C/350°F/gas mark 4. Put a 25cm (10in) loose-bottomed tart tin on a baking tray and surround it with a roll of crumpled foil to support the pastry.
4 To make the tart case, work with 2 sheets of filo at a time, keeping the others under a damp cloth. Brush the sheets lightly with butter and arrange them in the tin. Place the sheets over each other at different angles to ensure the base is evenly covered. The corners will hang over the edges of the tin at intervals.
5 Pour in the filling and shake the tin to distribute it evenly. Bake for about 40 minutes. Serve the tart either hot or warm.

MOORISH AUBERGINES

INGREDIENTS

2 medium aubergines
2 cloves garlic, crushed
handful of flat-leaf parsley leaves
handful of basil leaves, including cinnamon
or holy basil if available
8 salted anchovy fillets
100g (3½oz) walnuts
5 tbsp red wine vinegar
approximately 150ml (¼ pint) olive oil
pinch cayenne pepper or ¼ tsp red pepper flakes

PREPARATION

1 Cut the aubergines in quarters lengthways and boil in salted water for 10–15 minutes, depending on size. Drain and plunge in a bowl of iced water. Leave for a few hours until the pieces become firm.
2 Put the garlic, parsley, basil, anchovies, walnuts and vinegar into a food processor and blend to a thick paste, scraping down the sides several times. While the machine is running, add enough oil to make a thick sauce. Season with cayenne.
3 Dry the aubergine quarters well on kitchen paper and arrange them on a flat dish. Cover with the sauce and leave overnight in the refrigerator.

STUFFED ARTICHOKES

Turkish cooking has a whole family of meatless dishes called "olive oil dishes". Leeks, celeriac, aubergines and beans are all delicious prepared this way, with or without stuffing. Illustrated overleaf. Serves 6.

INGREDIENTS

3 lemons
2 tbsp plain flour
6 medium artichokes
salt
3 tbsp olive oil
1 tsp sugar
Stuffing
6 tbsp olive oil
3 medium onions, finely chopped
1 tbsp unsalted pistachio or pine nuts
60g (2oz) long-grain rice
salt and black pepper
1 tsp ground allspice
30g (1oz) chopped flat-leaf parsley
30g (1oz) chopped dill
30g (1oz) chopped mint
lemon slices and dill, to garnish

PREPARATION

1 Mix together the juice of 1 lemon and the flour with 250ml (8fl oz) water in a bowl and keep nearby as you prepare the artichokes.
2 Cut off the artichoke stalks and outer leaves. Bend back the inner leaves and snap them near the bottom, leaving the fleshy part attached to the base. The fresher the artichokes, the easier they will snap; cut the leaves if necessary. Slice off the innermost leaves just above the base and scoop out completely the fuzzy chokes. As you clean each artichoke, rub it with half a lemon sprinkled with salt to prevent discoloration and put it into the lemon-flour-water mixture.
3 To make the stuffing, heat the oil in a heavy pan and sauté the onions. Add the nuts and cook until they turn golden, then stir in the rice. Season with salt, pepper and allspice and sauté for a further 5 minutes. Add 150ml (¼ pint) boiling water, cover and simmer for 10–15 minutes, or until the rice is almost tender and the water has been absorbed. Take the pan off the heat and stir in the chopped parsley, dill and mint.
4 Remove the artichokes from the liquid, setting it to one side, and stuff them with the rice and nut mixture. Arrange them in a single layer in a flame-proof casserole. Add the reserved lemon-flour-water mixture and 3 tablespoons olive oil, pouring it between the vegetables and the side of the pan.

5 Sprinkle over the sugar. Put a sheet of moistened greaseproof paper over the artichokes. Put on the lid and cook over a medium heat for 10 minutes. Reduce the heat to very low and simmer for about 1 hour. If you prefer, they can be cooked in the oven at 180°C/350°F/gas mark 4.
6 Leave the artichokes to cool in the casserole. Lift them out on to a platter and serve cold, garnished with lemon slices and dill.

GRATIN OF FENNEL

A good main dish for a vegetarian meal, or an accompaniment to roast meat or baked fish.
Illustrated on page 111.

INGREDIENTS

4 bulbs Florence fennel
6 tbsp olive oil
1 medium onion, sliced
2 cloves garlic, sliced
400g (13oz) tomatoes, skinned, deseeded and chopped
1 tbsp chopped winter savory
2 tbsp chopped lemon balm
salt and black pepper
1 glass dry white wine
5 tbsp coarse dried breadcrumbs

PREPARATION

1 Remove the outer leaves of the fennel and slice the bulbs thickly. Heat 4 tablespoons of the olive oil and gently sauté the onion and garlic. Add the fennel and let the pieces colour lightly, turning them from time to time with a wooden spoon. Do not let any of the vegetables burn.
2 Heat the oven to 200°C/400°F/gas mark 6.
3 Add the tomatoes and herbs, season with salt and pepper and simmer for 5 minutes.
4 Transfer all the vegetables to a gratin dish. Deglaze the pan with the wine over a high heat, then pour the wine over the fennel. Scatter the breadcrumbs on top and drizzle over the remaining oil. Bake for 20 minutes.

Purslane and
Spinach Salad
(see page 112)

Stuffed Artichokes
(see previous page)

Gratin of Fennel
(see page 109)

SALADS

A bouquet of fresh herbs is essential when composing a salad: even a few parsley leaves will enliven the flavours. Add herbs to vinaigrettes, to cream and yogurt dressings, or use them to aromatize the oil or butter for croûtons. Some salad herbs, such as rocket and dandelion, are excellent with fruit; a final scattering of flowers produces a combination that is hard to resist.

PURSLANE AND SPINACH SALAD

Try to get a piece of feta cheese that is not too salty; some salt can be drawn out by soaking it in water for a few hours. Illustrated on page 110.

INGREDIENTS

100g (3½oz) young spinach leaves
100g (3½oz) purslane sprigs
handful of young nasturtium leaves or salad burnet
100g (3½oz) feta cheese, drained weight
nasturtium flowers
2 tbsp walnut oil
3 tbsp olive oil
2 tbsp herb vinegar
black pepper

PREPARATION

1 Arrange the spinach, purslane and nasturtium leaves in a salad bowl.
2 Crumble the feta cheese over them and top with the nasturtium flowers.
3 Whisk the walnut and olive oil with the vinegar to make a dressing and season with pepper. Spoon it over the salad.

MINT, CARROT AND HAMBURG PARSLEY SALAD

This recipe comes from Culinary and Salad Herbs *by Eleanour Sinclair Rohde, published in 1940. The original recipe calls for no oil, but a tablespoonful may be added. Lovage is a good alternative to mint, but use less, about 60g (2oz). I have also made the salad with grated celeriac instead of Hamburg parsley, to good effect. Remember to grate white roots at the last minute to avoid discoloration. Serves 2.*

INGREDIENTS

1 small onion, finely sliced
100g (3½oz) mint leaves
2 heaped tbsp grated carrot
2 heaped tbsp grated Hamburg parsley root
lemon juice, to taste
salt and black pepper

PREPARATION

1 Pound the onion and mint together or blend briefly in a food processor.
2 Stir in the carrot and Hamburg parsley root and dress with lemon juice, salt and pepper.

GREEN BEAN AND MUSHROOM SALAD

INGREDIENTS

200g (7oz) French beans, topped and tailed
100g (3½oz) mushrooms
3 tbsp sunflower oil
2 tbsp light soy sauce
2 tbsp rice or wine vinegar
salt and black pepper
a few Chinese chives, cut in short lengths
2–3 rao ram leaves or a few coriander or water celery leaves, shredded

PREPARATION

1 Put the French beans into boiling water and cook until barely tender, then drain them. Quarter the mushrooms.
2 Heat a wok and when it is very hot pour in 2 tablespoons of the oil. Add the mushrooms and stir-fry them quickly, then add the beans and stir-fry for one minute longer.
3 Whisk together the remaining oil, soy sauce and vinegar. Season the dressing with salt and pepper.
4 Put the vegetables into a bowl and scatter over the herbs. Pour on the dressing and toss the salad so that the mushrooms and beans are well coated.

PEAR AND RASPBERRY SALAD

This recipe comes from Angelo Lancellotti of the renowned Da Lancellotti restaurant in Soliera, near Modena in Italy. Illustrated above.

INGREDIENTS

4 tbsp raspberries
3 Williams' pears
handful of rocket leaves, coarsely chopped
1–2 sprigs of tarragon, finely chopped
1–2 tbsp virgin olive oil
1 tbsp balsamic vinegar
violet and borage flowers

PREPARATION

1 Squash the raspberries with the back of a fork. Slice the pears at the last moment to prevent them turning brown.
2 Mix the herbs and fruit, letting the raspberries coat the pears. Add the olive oil, then the vinegar and toss. Scatter the flowers on top and serve.

APPLE, DANDELION AND NASTURTIUM SALAD

Another original salad from Angelo Lancellotti.

INGREDIENTS

3 Reinette or Cox's apples
lemon juice
small bunch chives
large handful of dandelion leaves
a few marjoram sprigs
2–3 tbsp virgin olive oil
1 tbsp balsamic vinegar
nasturtium and marjoram flowers

PREPARATION

1 Slice the apples and paint them with a little lemon juice to stop any discoloration.
2 Cut the chives, and dandelion leaves if necessary, into short lengths and chop the marjoram leaves, not too finely. Combine the herbs and apple slices.
3 Dress with oil and vinegar and add the flowers.

DAIKON AND KIWI FRUIT SALAD

Illustrated on page 58.

INGREDIENTS

1 daikon (mooli) radish, weighing about 250g (8oz)
1 tbsp lemon juice
3 kiwi fruit, ripe but still firm
4 tbsp sunflower oil
2 tsp sesame oil
2 tbsp rice vinegar
2 tsp light soy sauce
salt
1 tbsp dry-roasted sesame seeds (see page 93)
a few purple and green basil leaves or perilla leaves,
or ½ box perilla sprouts

PREPARATION

1 Peel the radish, slice thinly and sprinkle with lemon juice to prevent discoloration. Peel and slice the kiwi fruit fairly thinly.
2 Make a dressing with the oils, vinegar, soy sauce and salt. Arrange the radish and kiwi fruit on a serving plate and scatter over the sesame seeds. Spoon over the dressing. Top with torn basil or perilla leaves, or perilla sprouts.

BROAD BEAN SALAD WITH PARMA HAM

A pleasant salad in which several herbs would work – calamint, chives, lemon balm or salad burnet. Using hazelnut oil and herb vinegar would be another way of making subtle flavour changes. Illustrated on page 59.

INGREDIENTS

350g (11½oz) small broad beans, shelled weight
4 tbsp olive oil
200g (7oz) red cherry tomatoes
4 slices Parma ham, cut into julienne strips
1 tbsp sherry vinegar
salt and black pepper
1 tbsp chopped fresh marjoram

PREPARATION

1 Cook the beans in boiling water for 3–5 minutes, until just tender. Drain and sprinkle with 1 tablespoon of the oil, and allow to cool. Cut the tomatoes in half.
2 Make a vinaigrette from the remaining oil and the vinegar. Season with salt and pepper.
3 Mix the vegetables with the ham in a shallow dish and dress with the vinaigrette. Scatter over the marjoram and serve.

PARSLEY AND TAHINI SALAD

An extremely versatile dish from the Lebanon. The salad is an excellent accompaniment to roast meats and hard-boiled eggs. Tahini is an oily paste made from crushed sesame seeds.

INGREDIENTS

350g (11½oz) flat-leaf parsley
1–2 cloves garlic
salt
200ml (7fl oz) tahini
juice of 1–2 lemons
4 tbsp water

PREPARATION

1 Cut or pluck the leaves from the parsley and discard the stalks. Keep the leaves whole.
2 Crush the garlic with a little salt. Blend the tahini, lemon juice and water to make the dressing. Add the garlic. Taste and add more salt or lemon juice if you wish.
3 Put the parsley leaves into a serving bowl. Pour over the dressing, mix well and serve.

VARIATIONS

With a little less parsley and tahini and more water, it makes a good dip to serve with bread or raw vegetables. With even less parsley and equivalent amounts of tahini and water (about 100ml/3½fl oz) it makes a fine sauce for chicken or grilled fish. Experiment to find the balance you prefer.

RED PEPPER SALAD WITH OLIVES AND ANCHOVIES

If possible, use a mixture of black, purple and dark green bruised-looking olives, to add variety of taste and colour to the salad. Illustrated on page 58.

INGREDIENTS

*4 red peppers
large handful of coriander leaves
4 tbsp olive oil
2 tbsp red wine vinegar
100g (3½oz) olives
8 anchovy fillets*

PREPARATION

1 Roast the peppers over a gas flame or under a grill until charred all over. Put in a plastic bag and leave for 10 minutes. This makes them easier to peel, as does holding them under running cold water. Cut the peeled flesh into strips.
2 Chop most of the coriander coarsely, but keep a few leaves whole. Mix the oil and vinegar together to make a vinaigrette.
3 Mix the peppers, olives and chopped coriander in a bowl, arrange the anchovies and whole coriander on top and dress with the vinaigrette.

MANGO, MINT AND PRAWN SALAD

Illustrated on page 58.

INGREDIENTS

*2 ripe mangoes
60ml (2fl oz) single cream
60ml (2fl oz) double cream
½–1 tsp garam masala
1–2 tbsp lime juice
20 tiger prawns or jumbo shrimps, cooked and peeled
3–4 sprigs of mint*

PREPARATION

1 Peel the mangoes and slice the flesh. Reserve the juice that runs from them and any flesh adhering to the stones, to use in the dressing.
2 Blend together the single and double cream, garam masala and lime juice. Very finely chop any bits of leftover mango flesh and add them to the dressing with the mango juice. Taste and adjust the quantities of garam masala and lime juice according to your preferences.
3 Arrange the fruit and prawns on a serving plate. Spoon the dressing over the salad. Shred the mint leaves and scatter them over the top.

HERB AND FLOWER SALAD

Most green salads benefit from the addition of herbs and you can also make a salad largely composed of herb leaves. Choose a mixture of strong and milder flavoured leaves from angelica, anise, anise hyssop, balm, the basils, bergamot, borage, burnet, caraway, chervil, chives, dandelion, hyssop, lovage, marsh mallow, the mints, mint-scented marigold, purslane, rocket, a small leaf or two of rue, sorrel and sweet cicely. Garnish with herb flowers such as bergamot, borage, marigold, micromeria, nasturtium, rosemary, sage, thyme or violets. Dress with a vinaigrette made with a herb vinegar or oil or try this cream dressing. (Illustrated on page 59.)

INGREDIENTS

Cream Dressing
*2 hard-boiled egg yolks
1 tsp Dijon mustard
black pepper and salt
6 tbsp (90ml) cream
1 tbsp vinegar, preferably herb vinegar*

PREPARATION

1 Pass the egg yolks through a sieve into a bowl. Add the Dijon mustard, pepper and a little salt and blend together.
2 Mix in the cream to make a smooth paste, then stir in the vinegar. Pour over the salad and toss.

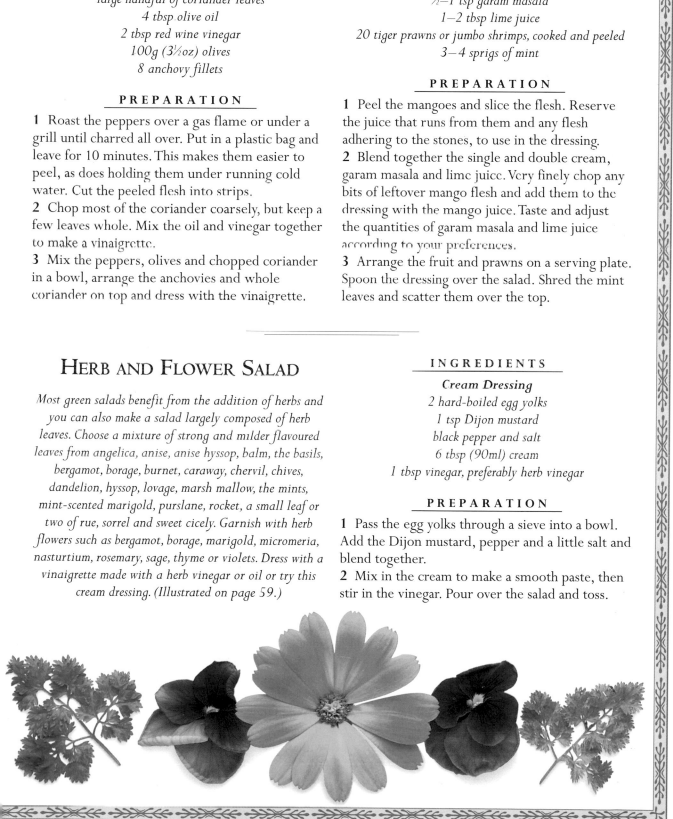

PASTA AND GRAINS

Grains are neutral and readily absorb flavours, so they benefit greatly from the addition of herbs. Pasta sauces and fillings are improved by a handful of herbs; rice flecked with green looks beautiful and can have a delicate or pungent taste according to the leaves chosen. Less widely used grains such as barley or bulgar wheat are also enhanced by herbs, although in their traditional cultures these may not be their regular companions.

LINGUINE WITH HERB SAUCE

The herbs for this sauce can be varied to include whatever is available, but they must be fresh. Aim for a harmonious blend of strong and more delicate flavours.

INGREDIENTS

1 young angelica leaf
4 stalks basil
4 stalks summer savory
2 stalks tarragon
1 stalk anise hyssop
2 young stalks lovage
3 stalks marjoram
2 sprays sweet cicely
6 sorrel leaves
handful of chervil or parsley
8–10 tbsp (120–150ml) virgin olive oil
3 tbsp chopped Welsh or spring onion
3–4 tbsp fresh breadcrumbs
500g (1lb) linguine
black pepper
freshly grated Parmesan, to serve

PREPARATION

1 Remove any thick stalks from the herbs and then chop them all coarsely.
2 Heat 2 tablespoons of the oil in a pan and sauté the Welsh onion and breadcrumbs until crisp.
3 Put the remaining oil into a large bowl and add all the herbs.
4 Meanwhile, bring a large pan of salted water to the boil and cook the linguine according to the instructions on the packet. Drain well and toss it in the oil and herb mixture.
5 Season with black pepper and scatter over the onion and breadcrumbs. Serve with some grated Parmesan to sprinkle over.

FARFALLE WITH ANGELICA AND PANCETTA

Farfalle, or pasta bows, are ideal with this sauce, but you can also use other shaped pasta such as shells or corkscrew-like fusilli. The angelica stems should be no thicker than a pencil or they may be tough and too strongly flavoured.

INGREDIENTS

2 shallots, chopped
30g (1oz) butter
4 thin stems angelica
100g (3½oz) pancetta or smoked lean bacon
400g (13oz) farfalle
1 tbsp hyssop leaves
150ml (¼ pint) single cream
salt and black pepper
1 tbsp olive oil

PREPARATION

1 Put the shallots in a pan to soften in the butter over a gentle heat. Cut the angelica stems into 1cm (½in) lengths and the pancetta into small cubes. Add them to the shallots and cook for a further 3–4 minutes.
2 Bring a pan of salted water to the boil for the farfalle. Cook it according to the instructions on the packet.
3 Add the hyssop and cream to the shallots, angelica and pancetta. Reduce the heat and cook, stirring constantly, until the cream is almost boiling. Add a little salt and lots of pepper. Cover and keep warm at the side of the stove.
4 When the pasta is cooked – it should remain *al dente* – drain and turn it into a serving bowl. Toss with olive oil, then pour over the sauce and serve.

FETTUCINE WITH PRAWNS AND TOMATO SAUCE

Tuna or swordfish, cut in cubes, makes an excellent alternative to prawns. Cook about 250–300g (8–10oz) in the sauce for 8–10 minutes.

INGREDIENTS

3 tbsp olive oil
20 large uncooked prawns, peeled
3 cloves garlic, finely sliced
2 tsp chopped lemon thyme
200ml (7fl oz) tomato passata
salt and black pepper
12 green olives, stoned and halved
1 red pepper, skinned, deseeded and sliced (see page 102)
400g (13oz) fresh fettucine
large handful of basil, shredded

PREPARATION

1 Heat 2 tablespoons of the oil in a frying pan and cook the prawns for 2–3 minutes until they curl and turn pink. Remove them and set aside. Add the garlic to the pan and cook gently until soft, but do not let it burn.

2 Meanwhile, heat a large pan of salted water for the fettucine.

3 Add the thyme to the garlic, then pour in the passata and season with salt and pepper. Simmer for a few minutes, then add the olives and red pepper. When the pasta water comes to the boil, reduce the heat under the sauce so that it barely bubbles and put back the prawns.

4 Cook the fettucine *al dente* according to the instructions, then drain. Put it into a serving bowl and toss with the remaining oil. Toss the basil into the sauce, pour it over the pasta and serve.

Pasta con le Sarde
Pasta with sardines

This is a traditional Sicilian dish, particularly popular in Palermo. The Sicilians use wild fennel, but garden fennel works well. The sardines must be fresh. Serves 6.

INGREDIENTS

750g (1½lb) fresh sardines
400g (13oz) green or bronze fennel
100g (3½oz) raisins
6 saffron threads
125ml (4fl oz) olive oil
1 large onion, finely chopped
6 anchovy fillets
100g (3½oz) pine nuts
500g (1lb) macaroni or bucatini

PREPARATION

1 Clean the sardines by scraping off the scales from tail to head with the back of a knife. Rinse in cold water, then slit along the length of the belly and take out the innards. Cut off the heads and tails and rinse again. To fillet them, open each fish by pressing your thumbs along the backbone to loosen it and free the flesh. Lift out the backbone together with the smaller bones.

2 Remove the thick stalks from the fennel and boil the leaves for 8–10 minutes in plenty of salted water. Drain, reserving the liquid to cook the pasta. Let the fennel cool and chop it coarsely.

3 Put the raisins to plump in hot water for 10 minutes. Crush the saffron in a little water.

4 Heat 2 tablespoons of the oil in a large pan and fry the onion until golden. Add the anchovy fillets and cook until softened. Stir in the pine nuts, drained raisins and saffron water. Cover and simmer for 10–15 minutes, adding a little more water if necessary.

5 Heat 3 tablespoons of oil in a second pan, put in half the sardines, crush with the back of a wooden spoon and cook to a paste, stirring frequently. Add the fennel and cook for a few minutes longer, then combine with the onion mixture.

6 Wipe out the pan, add 3 tablespoons of oil and fry the remaining sardine fillets on both sides until golden. They are rather fragile, so take care when turning them. Drain on kitchen paper or a rack.

7 Heat the oven to 190°C/375°F/gas mark 5. Bring the fennel water to the boil again and cook the pasta *al dente*. Drain and toss with the sauce. Put half the macaroni into an ovenproof dish, cover with a layer of fried sardines and top with the rest of the pasta. Cover the dish and bake for 15 minutes. Serve hot or cold.

Olive oil

Saffron

Raisins

Fennel

Sardines

Onion

Anchovy fillets

Pine nuts

Macaroni

LEEK AND HERB RISOTTO

*The herbs for this aromatic risotto can be
varied to suit your own taste, but make sure you
have a balance between the lighter and
stronger tasting kinds.*

INGREDIENTS

4 young leeks
60g (2oz) butter
1 clove garlic, chopped
1 tbsp chopped parsley
1 tbsp chopped sage
1 tbsp chopped sweet cicely
1 tbsp chopped marjoram
1 tsp chopped hyssop
1 tsp chopped rosemary
1 tsp chopped thyme
475g (15oz) carnaroli or arborio rice
approx 1¼ litres (2 pints) hot chicken or vegetable stock
12 green olives, pitted and chopped
1 tbsp chopped basil
30g (1oz) freshly grated Parmesan
salt and black pepper

PREPARATION

1 Clean the leeks and slice them fairly finely. Melt half the butter in a large heavy pan and cook the leeks and garlic over a gentle heat for about 5 minutes, stirring frequently. Add all the herbs (except the basil), let the flavours blend for a minute or two, then put in the rice and stir to coat all the grains with butter.

2 Raise the heat to medium and pour in a ladleful of hot stock. Stir constantly to ensure the rice does not stick to the pan and the liquid is distributed evenly. When this has been absorbed, add another ladleful of stock, keep stirring, and continue in this way until the rice is tender and has a creamy consistency.

3 Keep testing the rice after it has been cooking for 20 minutes to see how much more stock is needed; different types of rice absorb liquid at different rates. During the last few minutes of cooking, take care not to add too much. (You may not need to use the full quantity.) Keep stirring regularly so that the rice does not stick to the bottom of the pan.

4 When the rice is cooked, stir in the remaining butter, the olives, basil and Parmesan. Season with a little salt if necessary, and generously with black pepper. Serve at once.

IRANIAN RICE WITH HERBS

*This is a beautiful dish, traditionally served at
the Noo Rooz, or New Year, festival which is celebrated
in March and marks the beginning of spring.
Fresh herbs give a good clean flavour, but Iranian
shops sell large bags of dried herbs
specially mixed for cooking rice. They are exceptionally
fragrant. You will need only 60–70g (2–2½oz)
dried herbs to season 500g (1lb) rice.
Serves 4–6.*

INGREDIENTS

500g (1lb) basmati rice
salt
2 bunches spring onions or 1 bunch spring
onions and 1 bunch chives
100g (3½oz) parsley
100g (3½oz) coriander
100g (3½oz) dill
100g (3½oz) butter

PREPARATION

1 Soak the rice for several hours in salted water, then drain. Add 1 tablespoon of salt to 2½ litres (4 pints) of water, bring to the boil and tip in the rice. Boil, uncovered, for 3–4 minutes, stirring from time to time with a wooden fork. The rice should still be quite firm. Drain and rinse with lukewarm water.

2 Chop the spring onions finely. Remove any large stalks from the herbs and chop them all finely. Mix together.

3 Rinse the pan and add half the butter. Let it melt, add 2–3 tablespoons of water and, when hot, cover the bottom of the pan with a layer of rice. Spread over a thinner layer of herbs. Repeat the layers, finishing with rice, and mound the layers into a pyramid.

4 Melt the remaining butter and pour it over the rice. Poke a hole down through the centre with the handle of a wooden spoon. Cover with a cloth, then the pan lid and steam over a very low heat for 30 minutes. The rice can be left for longer, and will keep hot for 20 minutes or so after the heat has been turned off, provided the cloth and lid are left in place.

5 To serve, toss the rice with a fork to blend in the herbs and heap up in a serving dish. A crisp golden crust should have formed on the bottom of the pan. Remove this with a spatula and serve it as an accompaniment. The rice goes well with pan-fried fish and with most meats.

BAKED POLENTA WITH MUSHROOMS

INGREDIENTS

150g (5oz) polenta (cornmeal)
4 tbsp chopped flat-leaf parsley
2 tbsp chopped oregano
4 tbsp olive oil
20g (¾oz) dried porcini or other mushrooms
1 onion, chopped
1 carrot, chopped
1 clove garlic, chopped
300g (10oz) fresh mushrooms, sliced
400g (13oz) tomatoes, skinned, deseeded and chopped
salt and black pepper
60g (2oz) freshly grated Parmesan
60g (2oz) butter

PREPARATION

1 Bring 600ml (1 pint) lightly salted water to the boil and tip in the polenta, stirring hard. When it comes back to the boil, reduce the heat and cook for 20 minutes, stirring from time to time.
2 Lightly sauté half the parsley and oregano in a tablespoon of oil and stir into the cooked polenta. Spoon it into a shallow rectangular baking tin to make a layer 1.5cm (¾in) thick. Leave to cool.
3 Put the dried mushrooms to soak in some warm water. Heat the oven to 180°C/350°F/gas mark 4.
4 Heat the remaining oil and sauté the onion, carrot and garlic, until the onion is soft. Add the fresh mushrooms and tomatoes. Season with salt, pepper and the rest of the oregano. Cook for about 10 minutes: the mushrooms should still be firm, but have given out their liquid.
5 Drain the dried mushrooms, chop them and add to the sauce. Cook for a further 5 minutes. Stir in the rest of the parsley.
6 Cut the polenta into squares and put a layer into a buttered ovenproof dish. Spread a layer of sauce over it and about half the Parmesan, then dot with butter. Repeat the layers, dotting the top liberally with butter. Bake in the oven for 20–25 minutes until the top is browned. Serve with a green salad.

RIGATONI WITH HERB SAUCE

INGREDIENTS

400g (13oz) rigatoni or pasta bows
100ml (3½fl oz) olive oil
30g (1oz) butter
2 anchovy fillets, finely chopped
2 cloves garlic
2 sage leaves
5–6 mint leaves
7–8 large basil leaves
leaves from 1 sprig rosemary
leaves from 1 sprig thyme
leaves from 1 sprig savory
handful of chervil
handful of flat-leaf parsley
salt and black pepper
freshly grated Parmesan, to serve (optional)

PREPARATION

1 Bring a large pan of water to the boil and cook the pasta as directed on the packet, then drain.
2 Heat the oil and butter in a large pan and gently cook the anchovies, stirring frequently, until they have melted and thickened the oil and butter.
3 Finely chop the garlic and all the herbs and add to the anchovies. Stir them gently over a low heat for 3–4 minutes to release their aroma.
4 Stir in the cooked pasta, and season with salt and pepper to taste. Scatter over some Parmesan when serving, if you wish.

ELINOR'S COUSCOUS AND VEGETABLE SALAD

INGREDIENTS

300g (10oz) chickpeas, soaked overnight
500g (1lb) couscous
approximately 5–7 tbsp (75–105ml) olive oil
300g (10oz) mushrooms, quartered
4 courgettes, halved lengthwise and sliced into half-rounds
6 spring onions, sliced
small bunch coriander, chopped
salt and black pepper

PREPARATION

1 Cook the chickpeas in unsalted water until tender, about 1–1½ hours, depending on their age. If you are in a hurry, use canned, draining and rinsing them well. Cook the couscous according to the instructions on the packet, dress with a little olive oil and leave to cool.
2 Sauté the mushrooms in 2–3 tablespoons of the oil. Then sauté the courgettes separately in another 2 tablespoons of oil.
3 Spread the couscous in the bottom of a serving dish and season with salt and pepper. Arrange the vegetables on top and scatter over the coriander.

DESSERTS

The use of herbs in desserts and cakes is perhaps unexpected, but scented geraniums, lavender and bay have a delicate yet persistent perfume that is ideal for custards, creams and ices. Other herbs, among them mint and tarragon, have a clean taste that adds a refreshing touch of sharpness to a sweet dish, and a few – sweet cicely, lemon verbena and lemon balm – marry well with fruit. Herb sugars make a good standby when fresh leaves or flowers are not in season.

CLAFOUTIS OF APRICOTS

This rustic dish from central France is most often made with cherries, but it is good with other fruit such as apricots or plums. The flavours of lemon verbena or balm also complement apricots; for plums, try mint. If you have a suitable herb sugar (see page 125), use it in the clafoutis.

INGREDIENTS

500g (1lb) ripe apricots
30g (1oz) butter
75g (2½oz) sugar
3 tbsp brandy or dark rum
2 tbsp finely chopped sweet cicely
250ml (8fl oz) single cream or milk
3 eggs
60g (2oz) plain flour, sifted
icing sugar and a sprig of lemon verbena or mint, to decorate

PREPARATION

1 Cut the apricots in half and remove the stones. Heat the butter in a large frying pan and cook the fruit lightly with 3 tablespoons of the sugar for 10 minutes. The apricots should still hold their shape.
2 Remove from the heat, add the brandy and the sweet cicely and leave to soak for 30 minutes.
3 Heat the oven to 200°C/400°F/gas mark 6. Transfer the apricots, cut side uppermost, to a shallow 1–1½ litre (1¾–2½ pint) ovenproof dish.
4 Blend the cream, remaining sugar, eggs, flour and juices from the fruit at high speed in a blender or food processor. Pour over the fruit and bake for 30–35 minutes until the clafoutis is puffed up and lightly browned.
5 Serve warm rather than hot, sprinkled with icing sugar and decorated with lemon verbena.

Sweet cicely

Brandy

Sugar

Butter

Apricots

Single cream

Eggs

Plain flour

Icing sugar

Lemon verbena

LAVENDER ICE-CREAM

An ice-cream with a rich, soft texture and a delicate yet distinct taste of lavender. Illustrated on page 126. Serves 4–6.

INGREDIENTS

200ml (7fl oz) water
200g (7oz) sugar
30 lavender flowers
4 egg yolks
300ml (½ pint) double cream
2 egg whites

PREPARATION

1 Put the water and sugar into a heavy pan and bring slowly to the boil. Simmer for 5 minutes and remove from the heat. Infuse the lavender in the syrup and leave until cool, then strain.
2 Whisk the egg yolks until pale and creamy. Pour in the syrup in a steady stream, still whisking.
3 Beat the cream until it holds soft peaks and stir into the mixture. Beat the egg whites until stiff and fold them in.
4 Turn the mixture into an ice-cream machine, churn for 15 minutes, then store in the freezer. If you do not have a machine, set the freezer to its lowest setting at the start. Pour the mixture into a shallow tray and freeze. When set around the sides and on the bottom, tip into a chilled bowl and beat vigorously. Return to the tray and freeze. Repeat once more to ensure no large ice crystals form.

ROSE GERANIUM ICE-CREAM

INGREDIENTS

300ml (½ pint) milk
12 rose-scented geranium leaves
3 egg yolks
75g (2½oz) caster sugar
300ml (½ pint) double or whipping cream

PREPARATION

1 Heat the milk almost to boiling, remove and infuse the geranium leaves for an hour.
2 Beat the egg yolks and sugar until thick and pale.
3 Strain the milk, discarding the leaves. Gently reheat it and beat a little into the egg yolks. Pour the egg mixture into the milk and return the pan to a low heat. Stir continuously until the custard is thick enough to coat the back of a spoon, but do not let it boil. Leave to cool.
4 Whip the cream lightly and fold into the custard. Freeze in a freezer or ice-cream machine, as above.

MINT AND TEQUILA TART

Spearmint is the best kind to use in this tart; the leaves must be young. Serves 4–6.

INGREDIENTS

Shortcrust Pastry
175g (6oz) plain flour sifted with a pinch salt
100g (3½oz) butter, cubed
1 egg
1–2 tbsp iced water
Filling
3 eggs
250g (8oz) cream cheese
100ml (3½fl oz) crème fraîche
60g (2oz) caster sugar
6 tbsp (90ml) tequila
4 tbsp chopped young mint leaves
a few small mint leaves, to decorate

PREPARATION

1 Make the pastry by rubbing the butter into the flour to obtain a crumb-like texture. Bind with the egg and a little water. Leave to rest for 30 minutes, then roll out and line a 25cm (10in) loose-bottomed tart tin. Set it on a baking tray. Heat the oven to 180°C/350°F/gas mark 4.
2 Combine the ingredients for the filling in a food processor. Taste and add more sugar if you wish.
3 Put the filling in the pastry case and bake for 20–25 minutes, until the tart is golden and has risen slightly. Serve warm, decorated with mint.

RASPBERRY FOOL WITH LEMON BALM

INGREDIENTS

4 sprigs lemon balm
2 tbsp vodka
500g (1lb) raspberries
100g (3½oz) caster sugar
150ml (¼ pint) double cream
lemon balm leaves, to decorate (optional)

PREPARATION

1 Strip the leaves from the lemon balm and leave to soak in the vodka for 3–4 hours.
2 Crush the raspberries with a fork, adding the caster sugar a spoonful at a time. If you prefer a smooth texture, blend the raspberries with the sugar in a food processor.
3 Strain the vodka and stir it into the fruit with the cream. Chill and serve decorated with a few small lemon balm leaves, if you wish.

STRAWBERRIES WITH WOODRUFF SABAYON

The sabayon must be whisked until chilled, otherwise it may separate. If you like this dish, try sabayon flavoured with a few lavender flowers to accompany blueberries. Illustrated on page 127. Serves 6.

INGREDIENTS

2 sprigs woodruff
150ml (¼ pint) white wine
3 egg yolks
100g (3½oz) caster sugar
50ml (1¾fl oz) orange juice
grated zest ½ orange
500g (1lb) strawberries

PREPARATION

1 Infuse the woodruff in the wine for 2–3 hours, then discard the sprigs.
2 Whisk the egg yolks and sugar together in a large bowl until thick and pale. Put the bowl over a pan of hot but not boiling water, so that the bottom of the bowl is immersed in the hot water. Keep whisking and add the wine. After a few minutes' more whisking, the mixture should become frothy and mousse-like.
3 Remove from the heat and whisk in the orange juice and zest.
4 Set the bowl over a bowl of ice cubes and continue whisking until the mixture is cold. Serve with the strawberries.

ORANGES WITH TARRAGON SYRUP

INGREDIENTS

6 oranges
100g (3½oz) sugar
150ml (¼ pint) water
6 sprigs tarragon

PREPARATION

1 Peel the oranges, removing all pith. Slice, and remove any pips. Put the oranges into a shallow serving bowl and pour over the juice that has escaped as they were cut.
2 Heat the sugar and water in a heavy pan. When the sugar has dissolved, simmer the syrup for 3 minutes. Infuse 5 of the tarragon sprigs and leave until lukewarm.
3 Chop the remaining tarragon leaves finely and scatter over the oranges. Strain over the syrup and leave until quite cool, but do not chill.

GERANIUM CREAM CHEESE WITH BLACKBERRIES

Illustrated overleaf. If using a coeur à la crème mould, quantities are sufficient to fill two.

INGREDIENTS

250g (8oz) cream cheese
2 egg whites, whipped
3 tbsp geranium-flavoured herb syrup (see below)
300g (10oz) blackberries

PREPARATION

1 Mix the cream cheese with the egg whites and syrup. Line a sieve or mould with damp muslin. Put in the cheese and fold the edges of the muslin over the top. Leave to drain over a deep bowl for a few hours in the refrigerator or in a cool place.
2 Turn out the cheese on to a serving plate and surround it with the blackberries.

HERB SUGAR

Many early cookery books have instructions for making herb sugars and syrups for flavouring desserts and cakes. Use strong-scented leaves or flowers, such as lavender, lemon balm, lemon verbena, mint, pineapple sage, rosemary, scented geraniums and violets.

INGREDIENTS

200g (7oz) caster sugar
60g (2oz) fresh herb leaves or flowers

PREPARATION

Put the herb in a muslin bag in the bottom of a jar and add the sugar. Leave in a warm place for 1–2 weeks, then pour off the sugar into another jar and discard the herb bag. The sugar keeps indefinitely.

HERB SYRUP

INGREDIENTS

200g (7oz) sugar
150ml (¼ pint) water
a few fresh herb sprigs, leaves or flowers

PREPARATION

Bring the sugar and water slowly to the boil in a heavy pan. Simmer for 3 minutes, and then pour into a jar. Immerse the herb in the syrup and cover the jar. After a week discard the herb and keep the syrup in the refrigerator for up to 3 weeks.

*Geranium Cream Cheese
with Blackberries
(see previous page)*

*Lavender Ice-cream
(see page 124)*

Strawberries with
Woodruff Sabayon
(see page 125)

DRINKS

Every culture has its herb teas, often taken for their medicinal or digestive properties. Fragrant tisanes have become popular as after-dinner drinks; chilled and poured over ice they are an excellent alternative to the fruit drinks of summer afternoons.

Pineapple Cup

MINT AND LEMON SHERBET

INGREDIENTS

300ml (½ pint) water
150g (5oz) sugar
large handful of mint leaves, coarsely chopped
4 cardamom seeds, crushed
juice of 1 lemon
still or sparkling water
ice cubes
sprigs of mint, to decorate

PREPARATION

1 Bring the water and sugar to the boil in a heavy pan and add the mint and cardamom. Simmer for 3–4 minutes, then remove the pan from the heat, cover and leave to cool. The mint and cardamom should be allowed to infuse for at least 2 hours.
2 Strain the mixture and add the lemon juice.
3 To serve, dilute the syrup with still or sparkling water to taste, pour it over the ice cubes in individual glasses and decorate with sprigs of mint.

PINEAPPLE CUP

Serves 6–8.

INGREDIENTS

1 large pineapple
600ml (1 pint) syrup, as for the mango frappé, right
juice of 1–2 limes
1 litre (1¾ pints) still or sparkling water
sprigs of pineapple sage

PREPARATION

1 Peel and core the pineapple and purée the flesh in a food processor. Bring the syrup to the boil and add it with the motor running, then the lime juice.
2 Leave the drink to cool, add the water and serve decorated with sprigs of pineapple sage.

MANGO FRAPPE

INGREDIENTS

500ml (16 fl oz) water
200g (7oz) sugar
3 ripe mangoes
juice of 1 lemon
sprigs of mint (apple mint is good)

PREPARATION

1 Make a light syrup by boiling together the water and sugar. Peel the mangoes, then put the flesh into a blender and purée coarsely. Pour in the boiling syrup with the motor still running, then the lemon juice.
2 Cool and freeze until the frappé is almost solid, but do not let it pass the pouring stage. Crush the mint with a pestle or wooden spoon and add it to the glasses with the frappé.

MAY BOWL

*This fresh summer drink from Germany is flavoured
with woodruff, picked before it flowers. Use it
sparingly, so the wine does not acquire too strong a
flavour. A non-alcoholic May bowl can be made using
homemade lemonade or apple juice.*

INGREDIENTS

*1 bottle white (preferably German) or sparkling wine
2 sprigs woodruff
2 oranges, peeled and sliced*

PREPARATION

Pour the wine into a bowl or large jug and add the
woodruff and oranges, with any juice from slicing
them. Infuse for 10 minutes, then remove the
woodruff and serve, over ice cubes if you wish.

MULLED WINE WITH SAGE

This warming wine is based on an old Hungarian recipe.

INGREDIENTS

*½ bottle red wine
2 tbsp torn sage leaves
strip of lemon peel
2–3 tbsp sugar, or to taste
1 cinnamon stick, broken into pieces
juice of 1 lemon, or to taste*

PREPARATION

Heat the wine gently with the sage, lemon peel,
sugar and cinnamon. Bring to the boil, then
remove from the heat and stir in the lemon juice.

HERB TEAS

Herb teas or tisanes can be made from a number of
wild and garden herbs. Per cup, you usually need
2 tablespoons of a fresh herb or 1 tablespoon if
dried, depending on the strength of the herb.
Infuse the herb for a few minutes in boiling water,
then strain. To make an iced tea, use half the
quantity of water, cool and pour over ice cubes.

Angelica, bergamot, borage, scented geraniums,
hyssop, lemon balm, lemon verbena, lovage, mint,
marjoram, rosemary, sage and pineapple sage,
sweet cicely, thyme and woodruff all make good
herb teas.

A good summer tea blend comprises equal parts
apple mint, bergamot and lemon verbena. Fresh
lemon balm makes a good tea and refreshing
cooler when lemon juice is added to taste.

MOROCCAN MINT TEA

*The preparation of tea is an art in Morocco: it is
made in a tall silver pot and served in small glasses.
Makes ¾ litre (1¼ pints).*

INGREDIENTS

*1½ tbsp green tea
handful of sprigs of Moroccan mint
150g (5oz) sugar
approximately 750ml (1¼ pints) boiling water*

PREPARATION

1 Put the green tea into the pot and pour on a
little boiling water. Swirl it around and then pour
it out again, keeping the leaves in the pot. This
helps to remove the dust from the tea and some of
the bitterness.
2 Add the sprigs of mint and the sugar to the pot
and pour in the boiling water. Leave to steep for
about 5 minutes. Be sure to push down any mint
that rises to the surface or it will give the tea an
unpleasant taste.
3 To serve, pour into small glasses and offer more
sugar, usually lump sugar, if necessary.

VARIATIONS

Moroccans also make infusions of herbs such as
lavender, lemon verbena and mint. These are
sweetened with sugar and drunk either hot or cold
as digestive aids.

*Moroccan
Mint Tea*

BREADS

A number of traditional breads, such as the Tuscan rosemary bread shown below, are flavoured with herbs, but there is plenty of opportunity for the home baker to experiment with different herbs and grains to produce an even wider range. For example, try adding fresh fenugreek to an Indian nan. If you have some herb bread left over, use it for making croûtons for salads and soups.

CORN BREAD WITH PARSLEY AND BASIL

Corn bread is quick to make and is best eaten hot as an accompaniment to a main dish.

INGREDIENTS

125g (4oz) fine cornmeal
50g (1½oz) plain flour
50g (1½oz) oatmeal
3 tsp baking powder
½ tsp salt
2 tbsp poppy seeds
2 tbsp chopped flat-leaf parsley
2 tbsp chopped basil
3 eggs, well beaten
200ml (7fl oz) milk
4 tbsp cream
60g (2oz) butter, melted

PREPARATION

1 Heat the oven to 200°C/400°F/gas mark 6.
2 Mix the cornmeal, flour, oatmeal, baking powder, salt and poppy seeds in a large bowl and stir in the herbs.
3 Add the eggs and milk and beat well with a wooden spoon to a thick batter. Stir in the cream and melted butter.
4 Liberally oil a 20–23cm (8–9in) cast-iron skillet, the traditional pan for cooking corn bread, or a similar sized baking or cake tin. Pour in the batter and bake for 15–18 minutes. When cooked, a skewer or toothpick inserted in the middle should come out clean.
5 Cut the corn bread into triangles or squares and fold in a napkin to keep warm. Any left over can be cut in half and toasted or fried.

Corn Bread

Arab Bread with Zahtar

ARAB BREAD WITH ZAHTAR

This bread is usually baked in flat rounds and the top sprinkled with zahtar, a Middle Eastern herb and spice mixture, or it may be coated with a paste of olive oil and zahtar. In this version I have folded the bread around the flavouring so that less is lost when you cut or break a piece. Sumac is a deep red-purple, coarse powder with a tart flavour, ground from dried sumac berries. It is sold in Middle Eastern shops.

INGREDIENTS

½ *packet easy-blend yeast or 7g (¼oz) ordinary dried yeast*
500g (1lb) strong white bread flour
1 tsp salt
approximately 400ml (14fl oz) warm water
5 tbsp olive oil
Zahtar
50g (1½oz) sesame seeds
50g (1½oz) fresh thyme or zahtar leaves (see page 14) or 25g (¾oz) dried
25g (¾oz) sumac

PREPARATION

1 If using easy-blend yeast, sprinkle it over the flour with the salt. Put ordinary dried yeast to prove in a little of the warm water until frothy, then stir it into the flour.

2 Add 4 tablespoons of the oil and enough warm water to mix to a thick batter. Continue to stir for a minute or two, then turn on to a floured surface and knead until the dough is supple and elastic, about 7–8 minutes.

3 Put the dough to rise in a lightly oiled bowl covered with clingfilm. It should double in volume in about 1½ hours.

4 To prepare the zahtar, lightly dry-roast the sesame seeds in a frying pan (for method, see page 93) and leave to cool. Chop the thyme or grind it in a mortar and mix with the sesame seeds, sumac and remaining olive oil.

5 Punch down the dough, knead it briefly, then roll out on a floured surface into an oblong twice as long as it is wide and about 5mm (¼in) thick. Spread the zahtar lengthways down the centre of the oblong and fold over one side to cover the filling. Press the edge down lightly to seal it. (The shape of the finished bread is something like a German stollen.)

6 Put the bread on a lightly oiled baking tray, cover and leave to rise again for 30 minutes.

7 Heat the oven to 200°C/400°F/gas mark 6.

8 Bake the loaf for 20 minutes, then reduce the heat to 160°C/325°F/gas mark 3 and bake for a further 20–25 minutes. When ready, the bread should sound hollow if tapped on the bottom. Cool on a wire rack.

Wholewheat Herb Bread (recipe overleaf)

Rosemary Bread (recipe overleaf)

WHOLEWHEAT HERB BREAD

The herbs in this bread can be changed to suit your taste, as can the quantities, but choose those that withstand heat well such as sage, oregano, savory, rosemary, lovage and micromeria. Add seeds if you wish – dill, fennel and caraway are all excellent in bread. Makes two 500g (1lb) loaves. Illustrated on previous page.

INGREDIENTS

750g (1½lb) wholewheat flour
250g (8oz) strong white flour
1 packet easy-blend yeast or 15g (½oz) ordinary dried yeast
1 tsp salt
approximately 600ml (1 pint) warm water
1 tbsp chopped thyme
2 tbsp chopped dill
2 cloves garlic, finely chopped
3 tbsp olive oil, plus some for greasing

PREPARATION

1 Mix the flours together and place in a very low oven for a few minutes. Remove and sprinkle on the easy-blend yeast with the salt. If using ordinary dried yeast, put it to prove in a little of the warm water; make a well in the centre of the flour and add the mixture when it froths.

2 Add the herbs, garlic and oil. Mix all well into the flour with enough of the warm water to make a firm yet sticky dough.

3 Knead the dough in the bowl until smooth and elastic, adding a little more flour if necessary. Do not overhandle it.

4 Rinse the bowl, oil it lightly and put back the ball of dough to prove, covered with oiled clingfilm, until doubled in bulk, about 1½–2 hours.

5 Turn out on to a lightly floured surface, punch it down and knead briefly. Cut in half and form into two cylinders. Place on oiled baking sheets or shape them to fit two oiled 500g (1lb) loaf tins, making sure that the seam is underneath. Cover with a cloth or more oiled clingfilm and leave to rise for 45–60 minutes, until the dough has almost doubled in bulk or reached the top of the tins.

6 Heat the oven to 200°C/400°F/gas mark 6.

7 Bake for 20 minutes, then reduce the heat to 180°C/350°F/gas mark 4 and bake for a further 25–30 minutes until the bread sounds hollow when tapped on the bottom. If you have trouble getting the loaves out of the tins, leave on a cooling rack for 10 minutes. If they then do not sound hollow when tapped, put back on the oven shelf for a few minutes. Cool on a rack.

ROSEMARY BREAD

This bread, pan di ramerino, can now be found all year round in Tuscany, but it was originally made for the week before Easter. Italian bakers usually sell rolls rather than whole loaves. These quantities are sufficient for two 500g (1lb) loaves. Illustrated on previous page.

INGREDIENTS

1 packet easy-blend yeast or 1 tbsp ordinary dried yeast
1kg (2lb) strong white flour
1 tsp salt
leaves from 2 sprigs rosemary, finely chopped
approximately 600ml (1 pint) warm water
4 tbsp olive oil, plus some for greasing
75g (2½oz) raisins
1 egg, lightly beaten

PREPARATION

1 If you are using easy-blend yeast, sprinkle it over the flour with the salt and the rosemary, and stir well. If you have ordinary dried yeast, put it to prove in a little of the warm water and add it to the flour, salt and rosemary when frothy. Make a well in the middle of the flour before adding the liquids – the yeast mixture (if using ordinary dried), the olive oil and enough of the remaining warm water to mix to a cohesive dough with a wooden spoon.

2 Turn out the dough on to a floured surface and knead by hand for about 10 minutes, or with the dough attachment of a food processor, until it is very pliable and elastic. Form it into a ball.

3 Rinse out the bowl, oil it lightly and put back the dough. Cover with oiled clingfilm and leave to rise until doubled in bulk, about 1–1½ hours.

4 Punch the dough down and knead in the raisins. Cut in half and shape the dough into two rounds. Leave to rise again on oiled baking sheets (loaves seam-side down) for 30 minutes.

5 Heat the oven to 220°C/425°F/gas mark 7.

6 Using a razor, slash the top of the loaves in the form of a cross. Brush the tops with egg, then bake loaves for about 30 minutes, until the bread sounds hollow when tapped on the bottom. Cool on a wire rack.

VARIATION

If you wish to make rolls, cut the dough into small pieces and roll into balls. They will need only 15–20 minutes' rising time and will take 8–10 minutes to bake.

ROTI

This Indian unleavened bread is made with a mixture of chapati or wholewheat flour and chickpea flour. The coriander can be replaced by fenugreek, if you prefer.

INGREDIENTS

200g (7oz) wholewheat flour
60g (2oz) chickpea (gram) flour
1 tsp salt
¼ tsp chilli powder or cayenne
2 tsp garam masala or ground cumin
3 tbsp chopped coriander leaves
2 tbsp ghee (clarified butter) or oil
100ml (3½fl oz) yogurt
3–4 tbsp water
ghee, to serve

PREPARATION

1 Sieve the flours together and add the salt, spices, coriander, ghee and yogurt. Mix well to a firm dough, then add enough water to make it pliable.
2 Knead on a floured surface for 8–10 minutes until smooth and elastic. Alternatively, make the dough in a food processor: put in the dry ingredients, add the oil and yogurt in a gentle stream while the motor is running, then drizzle in enough water to form the dough into a smooth ball. Process for a few seconds more before removing the dough.
3 Let the dough rest in a lightly oiled bowl, covered with clingfilm, for an hour or so. Knead again briefly, then divide into 10–12 pieces. Shape into balls and keep covered with a cloth.
4 Roll them out on a floured surface into circles 12–15cm (5–6in) in diameter and 2.5mm (⅛in) thick. Rotate the discs as you roll them to get an even thickness. Cover the breads with a cloth.
5 Heat a griddle or heavy frying pan (with no fat) and cook each roti until the underside is dry and has blisters. Turn it and cook until brown spots show on the surface.
6 To puff up the bread, heat a back burner and put a heat diffuser over it. Put the roti on to the diffuser and it will puff up instantly – a matter of seconds. Remove to a basket lined with a tea towel and brush lightly with ghee. Fold over the cloth and keep warm.
7 Bake the other breads, removing the griddle or frying pan from the heat periodically so that it does not get too hot.
8 Serve warm with Lentils with Oriental Herbs (see page 105), chutneys and a glass of lassi, the Indian yogurt drink.

FOCACCIA

Focaccia is an easy bread to make and can be flavoured with a number of aromatic herbs. I have used sage here, but thyme, oregano and rosemary are suitable, too. For the last two reduce the amount to 2 tablespoons. It is best eaten on the day it is made. Makes 1 focaccia.

INGREDIENTS

½ packet easy-blend yeast or 7g (¼oz) ordinary dried yeast
375g (12oz) strong white flour
250ml (8fl oz) warm water
1 tsp salt, plus coarse salt for finishing
4 tbsp finely chopped fresh sage
2–3 tbsp olive oil

PREPARATION

1 Sprinkle easy-blend yeast over the flour, or, if using ordinary dried yeast, leave it to prove in the warm water.
2 Mix the salt and sage thoroughly with the flour. Add a tablespoon of oil and the water and mix to a soft dough. Remove the dough from the bowl to a floured surface and knead until it becomes springy and elastic.
3 Rinse the mixing bowl and oil it lightly. Return the dough and leave it to rise, covered with clingfilm, for about 50 minutes, or until it has doubled in bulk.
4 Heat the oven to 190°C/375°F/gas mark 5.
5 Lightly oil a baking sheet. Punch the dough down, knead it a little in the bowl, then form it into a ball. Put it in the centre of the baking sheet and spread it out with your hands to make a circle 2.5cm (1in) thick. Make some indentations in the surface with your fingers and leave to rise again for 20 minutes, covered with a cloth.
6 Brush the top with olive oil, sprinkle over a little coarse salt and bake for 40 minutes. When it is ready, the focaccia will sound hollow if tapped on the bottom. Cool on a wire rack.

HERB MIXTURES, MARINADES, RELISHES AND SAUCES

STORING HERBS

Fresh herbs will keep for a week or more in the refrigerator if packed, not too densely, in an airtight plastic box. They can also be put in plastic bags in the salad compartment, but do not crush the leaves. If you have a bunch of herbs you are going to use in a short time, put them in a jug of water in the kitchen and enjoy their fragrance.

Freezing is one of the most successful methods for preserving herbs. Wash and dry them in a salad spinner and with kitchen paper, then chop the leaves and store in small plastic pots or freeze them into ice cubes to store in plastic bags. Most herbs freeze well and retain their fragrance, although they look soft and wilted.

Drying is the traditional method of preserving herbs for winter; it is particularly suitable for those grown in hot climates, with more intense aromas. Pick the herbs early in the day, remove old or discoloured leaves and tie in bunches. Hang in a warm place, out of direct sunlight, until the leaves feel dry and crumble if rubbed. Strip the leaves and store them in jars. A microwave is the most efficient way of drying herbs. Wash and dry the herbs as above and scatter two handfuls of leaves or sprigs evenly on thick kitchen paper. Microwave at 100 per cent for 4 minutes. Bay leaves may take slightly longer. Leave to cool, then store in jars. When drying herbs, fennel, lovage, mint, rosemary, sage, savory, tarragon and thyme are best picked before flowering; hyssop, marjoram and oregano should be picked in flower.

Garlic purée Cover 6 whole garlic heads with boiling water. Simmer 15–20 minutes until soft. Drain and leave to cool, remove the skins and blend in a food processor or pass through a fine sieve. Add a little salt and 4 tablespoons olive oil. Put into a jar, pour over 4 tablespoons olive oil to seal. Cover with an airtight lid and refrigerate. Use to flavour soups, sauces and vegetable purées. It goes well with roast lamb, or can be spread on toast and topped with chopped herbs or tomatoes.

FRESH HERB MIXTURE

Stir into vegetable stews, or rub on to lamb or pork.

INGREDIENTS

small sprig rue
2 sprigs mint
2 sprigs oregano
2 sprigs thyme
3–4 lovage leaves
6 sprigs parsley

Purée the herbs in a mortar; the mixture will keep for 2–3 days in the refrigerator.

HERBES DE PROVENCE

Use in daubes (braised meat dishes), game dishes and with root vegetables.

INGREDIENTS

4 tbsp dried thyme
2 tbsp dried marjoram
1 tbsp dried rosemary
2 tbsp dried savory
1 tbsp dried lavender flowers
1 tbsp dried hyssop
3 bay leaves

Grind all the herbs together. Sieve them and then store in an airtight jar.

FRENCH MIXTURE

Use with fish, chicken, lentils and mushrooms.

INGREDIENTS

2 tbsp dried tarragon
2 tbsp dried winter savory
2 tbsp dried marjoram
2 tbsp dried thyme

Grind the ingredients together, sieve and store in an airtight jar.

Bouquet for Poultry   *Bouquet for Game*   *Bouquet for Meat*

BOUQUETS GARNIS

A bouquet garni is a little bundle of herbs used to flavour slowly cooked dishes. The herbs are tied with a long string so that they are easily removed at the end of cooking, or they can be enclosed in muslin. A standard bouquet is made up of a few sprigs of thyme, a bay leaf and 2–3 fresh parsley stalks, but it can be varied to suit the dish and the inclinations of the cook. Here are a few suggestions.

Three variations for fish
Tarragon, thyme, parsley and lemon peel.
Fennel, bay and lemon thyme.
Dill, spring or Welsh onions, parsley and mint.
Three variations for poultry
Parsley, bay, tarragon and bruised lemon grass.
Summer savory, marjoram and rosemary.
Thyme, sage, allspice and lemon peel.
Five variations for meat
Parsley, thyme, garlic and bay.
Lovage, parsley and lemon thyme.
Oregano, orange peel, thyme and bay.
Rosemary, mint, winter savory and marjoram.
Celery, Hamburg parsley, thyme and sage.
Two variations for game
Parsley, juniper berries, thyme and bay.
Rosemary, orange peel, marjoram and balm.

HERB GARNISHES

To add a crisp, fresh taste to a dish, a southern European cook will stir in or scatter over a finely chopped aromatic garnish just before serving. This will enliven any plainly cooked meat, fish, grain or vegetable dish, or lift a winter soup or stew. In France it would be a *persillade*, in Italy a *gremolata*. The latter is the classic addition to *ossobuco* but the lemon zest gives it a liveliness that suits oily fish as well. Many Catalan recipes are finished with a *picada*, which also thickens the dish.

Persillade Chop finely together a handful of flat-leaf parsley and 2 cloves of garlic.
Gremolata Chop and mix together a handful of flat-leaf parsley, 2 cloves of garlic and the grated rind of half a lemon.
Picada Pound or blend together 2 cloves of garlic, a handful of flat leaf parsley, 60g (2oz) toasted hazelnuts, almonds or pine nuts, 1 tablespoon toasted breadcrumbs (optional), pinch of saffron (optional), then thin the mixture with a little stock from the dish, sherry or water. Stir in before serving.

FRIED HERB SPRIGS

These make a splendid nibble, or an accompaniment to meat, fish and omelettes. Curled parsley, chervil, sage and chives – especially Chinese chives, cut in short lengths – are all good. They must be eaten straight away.

PREPARATION

1 Pick the herbs just before frying, and wash and dry them thoroughly.
2 Heat some oil to about 160°C/325°F in a deep fryer (if it gets too hot the herbs will burn). Put in a few sprigs at a time, in a frying basket or loose.
3 Lift out the herbs as soon as they stop sizzling – they should be ready after about 1 minute – and drain them on kitchen paper.

HERB VINEGARS

Herb vinegars are useful for dressings, sauces and marinades. Use fresh herbs, picked early in the day before the sun draws out the aromatic oils, and wine, cider or rice vinegar. Most flowering herbs are milder than those picked earlier in the season, but flower sprigs can be put into the finished bottles for their decorative effect.

To make herb vinegars, use approximately 60g (2oz) of the herb to 500ml (16fl oz) vinegar. Crush the sprigs or leaves to bring out their flavour, put them in a glass jar and cover with vinegar. Leave to steep for three weeks (the flavours develop more quickly if kept in the sun), then strain the vinegar into bottles. Put a fresh sprig of the herb into each bottle – it strengthens the flavour as well as serving as identification. Use bottles with corks or plastic-lined caps. Vinegars will keep for several years, becoming mellower and sweeter as they age.

Suitable herbs: basil, borage, burnet, chives, dill, garlic, lavender, lemon balm, lemon verbena, mint, nasturtium flowers, rosemary, tarragon, thyme and violets. Chillies, lemon zest, peppercorns and seeds of coriander, dill, fennel and mustard can be used as additional flavourings.

Lemon vinegar: use a mixture of lemon balm, lemon thyme, lemon verbena, crushed lower part of 2–3 lemon grass stalks and peel of 2 lemons.

Garrigue vinegar: use a mixture of winter savory, thyme, rosemary and bay leaves with 1–2 cloves of garlic and 1–2 dried chillies.

Summer salad vinegar: use a combination of basil, borage, chives and tarragon.

HERB OILS

The best herbs to use are basil, bay, dill, fennel, garlic, lemon grass, mint, oregano, rosemary, savory and thyme. Dried chillies or peppercorns and the seeds of anise, cumin, dill or fennel may be added.

To make herb oils, use 3–4 tablespoons or 4–6 sprigs of the herb to 500ml (16fl oz) oil. Use virgin olive, light sunflower or grapeseed oil. Put the herbs in a glass jar, pour over the oil, close and leave in a warm place for 2–3 weeks. Strain into a clean bottle and label. Herb oils will keep for up to a year if stored in a cool, dark place.

HERB BUTTERS

These can accompany grilled fish, poultry or meat and most vegetables, and are good for making sandwiches. Many herbs make successful butters. Serve basil butter with baked or grilled tomatoes or mushrooms; burnet butter enlivens a dish of lentils; chive butter is a good accompaniment for peas and mangetouts. Dill or fennel butter goes well with any fish or with a dish of flageolets, marjoram butter with kidney beans or broccoli, mint and mint-scented marigold with carrots, peas and grilled lamb. Parsley (*maître d'hotel*) butter is traditionally served with grilled steak and is excellent with courgettes; tarragon butter can accompany salsifies or pumpkin. A butter made with a mixture of dill and lemon verbena goes well with courgettes, green beans or fish.

To make herb butters, soften 150g (5oz) butter with a fork, beat in 1–2 tablespoons lemon juice and 4–6 tablespoons chopped herbs. When well blended, shape the butter into a long roll, wrap in foil and refrigerate until needed. Herb butters can be frozen for a few months. You can also try adding paprika, cayenne, ground pepper, garlic or shallot.

Herb Oil and Garrigue Vinegar

MARINADES

Marinades are an important element in preparing meat or fish to be grilled, roasted or fried; they tenderize and enhance flavour and also help to preserve the food. They are usually liquid, but Latin American and Mexican cooks also use pastes, called *adobos*, which are rubbed on to the food.

To marinate food, mix the marinade ingredients together in a container that will not react with acid (for instance glass or ceramic). Immerse the meat or fish, turning it from time to time. Put the food in the refrigerator, but bring it to room temperature before cooking. Meat should be marinated for 3–4 hours and can stand overnight; fish and shellfish need only 1–2 hours. Use the marinade to baste the food while cooking. To serve it as a sauce, first bring it to the boil to kill any bacteria from the raw meat or fish. A marinade should never be re-used.

CHIMICHURRI

This marinade and sauce for grilled meat comes from Argentina, where it is most commonly used with steaks. Marinate the meat in some of the chimichurri, reserving the rest to serve as a sauce.

INGREDIENTS

4 cloves garlic, finely chopped
1 tsp black peppercorns, crushed
2 tsp oregano leaves
1 bay leaf, crumbled
6 tbsp chopped flat-leaf parsley
1–2 tsp chilli flakes
100ml (3½fl oz) olive oil
80ml (2½fl oz) red wine herb vinegar

AN ORIENTAL MARINADE

Use for spare ribs, poultry or fish.

INGREDIENTS

6 tbsp (90ml) rice wine vinegar
150ml (¼ pint) fish sauce
juice of 2 limes
4 tbsp sunflower oil
2 shallots, chopped
2 cloves garlic, chopped
small piece of fresh ginger, chopped
2 tsp sugar
1 fresh chilli, sliced, or 1 dried chilli, crushed
4 tbsp chopped coriander – root, leaf and stalk

RED WINE MARINADE

Use for game and large cuts of meat. In Germany, a few sprigs of woodruff might replace the rosemary and thyme.

INGREDIENTS

½ bottle red wine
1 tbsp olive or sunflower oil
1 sprig rosemary
2–3 stalks thyme
2 bay leaves
1 onion, sliced
4 allspice berries, crushed

YOGURT MARINADE

Use for lamb or beef that is to be grilled.

INGREDIENTS

300ml (½ pint) plain yogurt
4 tbsp olive or sunflower oil
1 clove garlic, crushed
1 small onion, grated
¼ tsp paprika or cayenne
2 tbsp each basil and mint

SEAFOOD MARINADE

The alcohol enhances the flavour of the fennel.

INGREDIENTS

150ml (¼ pint) white wine
3 tbsp lemon juice
3 tbsp Pernod, ouzo or dry anís
3 tbsp olive or sunflower oil
handful of fresh fennel leaves and stalks

A NEW MEXICAN ADOBO

Use for pork, beef or fillets of firm-fleshed fish. Purée all the ingredients in a food processor.

INGREDIENTS

6–8 dried chillies, toasted (see page 92)
4 cloves garlic, chopped
1 small onion, chopped
a few black peppercorns, crushed
2 bay leaves, crumbled
1 tbsp dried Mexican or European oregano
2 tsp thyme
juice of 1 orange
juice of ½ lemon

SALSAS, RELISHES, CHUTNEYS AND SAUCES

These all provide a good way of adding the flavours of herbs to plainly cooked foods, such as poached fish or grilled meat. Several of the salsas and sauces included in preceding recipes can be used with other dishes, for instance the herb and horseradish sauces, page 79; salsa cruda, page 84; salsa fresca, page 92; lemon balm salsa, page 93; béarnaise and paloise sauces, page 101.

PARSLEY, ONION AND ORANGE SALSA

A refreshing salsa for roast or grilled meats.

INGREDIENTS

60g (2oz) curly parsley, chopped
1 small red onion, chopped
1 clove garlic, chopped
juice of 2 oranges
juice of 2 lemons
4 tbsp olive oil

PREPARATION

Mix all the ingredients together. The salsa can be kept, covered, in the refrigerator for up to 2 days.

RED PEPPER RELISH

This relish from the Balkans usually accompanies meats or fried fish but it is also good spread on crusty bread or as a topping for bruschetta. A mixture of red and yellow peppers may be used.

INGREDIENTS

6 large cloves garlic
2 onions, quartered
6 red peppers, skinned and deseeded (see page 102)
thinly grated rind of 1 lemon
100g (3½oz) flat-leaf parsley, chopped
200ml (7fl oz) sunflower oil
60ml (2fl oz) red wine vinegar

PREPARATION

Blanch the garlic and onions in boiling water, then drain well and chop. Chop the red peppers and mix with the garlic and onions. Add the lemon rind and parsley. Whisk the oil and vinegar together and pour over the peppers. Mix well, then pour into a clean bowl or jar and chill for several hours. The relish will keep for up to a week in the refrigerator.

LOVAGE AND LIME RELISH

An ideal relish for grilled fish, chicken or pork.

INGREDIENTS

5 tbsp chopped lovage
1½ tsp ground cumin seeds
1–2 green chillies, deseeded and chopped
5 tbsp lime juice
4 tbsp olive oil

PREPARATION

Combine all the ingredients. The relish will keep, if covered, for up to 2 days in the refrigerator.

CORIANDER CHUTNEY

A fresh, sharp-tasting chutney to serve as an accompaniment to Indian dishes.

INGREDIENTS

250g (8oz) coriander leaves and young stalks
1–2 green chillies, deseeded and chopped
2 cloves garlic, chopped
60g (2oz) sesame seeds, dry-roasted (see page 93)
30g (1oz) sugar
2 tsp salt
250ml (8fl oz) white wine vinegar

PREPARATION

Put the coriander, chillies, garlic and sesame seeds into a food processor and blend. Scrape down the sides of the container from time to time. Add the sugar, salt and vinegar and blend again until incorporated. Sealed in a container, the chutney can be stored in the refrigerator for a few weeks.

PESTO

This vivid green sauce has become a classic. You can use different basils; lemon basil and African Blue basil are particularly successful. Alternatively, try replacing the basil with coriander, mint or rocket, and the pine nuts with walnuts. Follow the instructions for making pistou on page 50, adding the nuts with the basil and garlic.

INGREDIENTS

6 large handfuls of basil leaves
3 tbsp pine nuts
3 cloves garlic, crushed with a little salt
60g (2oz) freshly grated Parmesan or pecorino cheese
approximately 180–200ml (6–7fl oz) olive oil

Lovage and Lime Relish

Frankfurt Green Sauce

Red Pepper Relish

FRANKFURT GREEN SAUCE

INGREDIENTS

150ml (¼ pint) olive oil
2–3 tbsp herb vinegar
1 tbsp Dijon mustard
100g (3½oz) mixed herbs such as borage, chervil,
chives, dill, parsley, salad burnet, savory, sorrel
and tarragon, finely chopped
salt and black pepper
1 tsp sugar
3 hard-boiled eggs, chopped

PREPARATION

Whisk together the oil, vinegar and mustard and
stir in the herbs. Season with salt, pepper and
sugar and add the egg. Serve with cooked meats,
baked or poached fish and salads.

SALSA VERDE

INGREDIENTS

1 bunch flat-leaf parsley
a few basil, mint or calamint leaves
1 clove garlic, crushed
4 anchovy fillets, chopped
1 tbsp capers, chopped
approximately 200ml (7fl oz) olive oil
salt and black pepper

PREPARATION

Put the herbs, garlic, anchovies and capers into a
food processor and blend with a few tablespoons
of oil. With the motor running, add the remaining
oil in a slow stream. Season to taste. Serve with
poached fish and boiled meats. In Italy, regional
variations may include other herbs, hard-boiled
egg yolks or breadcrumbs soaked in vinegar.

SAUCE MESSINE

INGREDIENTS

1 lemon
2 tbsp chopped chervil
2 tbsp chopped parsley
2 tbsp chopped tarragon
2 shallots, chopped
300ml (½ pint) cream
30g (1oz) butter
2 egg yolks

PREPARATION

Grate the rind of half the lemon and mix with the
herbs and shallots. Put the mixture into a heavy
pan or the top of a double boiler with the cream,
butter and egg yolks. Heat gently, whisking all the
time, for 10–15 minutes, until the sauce thickens.
Do not let it boil. Squeeze the lemon and stir in
the juice to taste. This sauce is an excellent
accompaniment to poached fish.

SALMORIGLIO

INGREDIENTS

150ml (¼ pint) olive oil
60ml (2fl oz) hot water
juice of 2 lemons
1 tsp dried or 1 tbsp fresh chopped oregano
2 tbsp chopped flat-leaf parsley
black pepper and salt

PREPARATION

Beat the oil in the top of a double boiler, gradually
adding the hot water. Whisk in the lemon juice and
herbs and season. Heat gently and beat well – the
sauce should be smooth. Pour over grilled fish,
roast meat or green vegetables.

INDEX

USEFUL ADDRESSES

Listed below are suppliers of some of the more unusual herbs and foods. Check opening times before visiting and send a stamped, addressed envelope if you need a reply.

SPECIALIST NURSERIES

Arne Herbs
Limeburn Hill
Chew Magna
Avon BS18 8QW
Tel: 01275 333399
Wide-ranging list includes epazote.

Cheshire Herbs
Fourfields
Forest Road
Nr Tarporley
Cheshire CW6 9ES
Tel: 01829 760578
Fax: 01829 760354
Excellent range, especially basils.

Iden Croft Herbs
Frittenden Road
Staplehurst
Kent TN12 0DH
Tel: 01580 891432
Excellent range.

Jekka's Herb Farm
Rose Cottage
Shellards Lane
Alveston
Bristol BS12 2SY
Tel: 01454 418878
Wide range includes oriental herbs. Plants and seeds by mail order.

Poyntzfield Herb Nursery
Black Isle, By Dingwall
Ross & Cromarty
Scotland IV7 8LX
Tel: 01381 610352
Unusual herbs. For mail order list, send 4 first-class stamps.

SEED SUPPLIERS

Suffolk Herbs
Monks Farm
Pantlings Lane
Kelvedon
Essex CO5 9PG
Fax: 01376 571189

ORIENTAL FOODS

Wing Yip branches at:
375 Neckells Park Road
Birmingham B7 5NT

395 Edgware Road
London NW2 6LN

Oldham Road
Manchester M4 5HU

550 Purley Way
Croydon
Surrey CR0 4RF
All stock a wide range.

Yaohan Oriental Shopping Centre
399 Edgware Road
London NW9 0JJ
Tel: 0181 200 0009
Japanese food, including herbs.

CENTRAL AND SOUTH AMERICAN FOODS

Cool Chile Co
P O Box 5702
London W11 2GS
Tel: 0973 311714
Huge range of chillies. Also tomatillo seeds.

Peppers by Post
Seaspring Farm
West Bexington
Nr Dorchester
Dorset DT2 9DD
Tel: 01308 897892
Chillies and tomatillos in season.

BIBLIOGRAPHY

Bond, R: articles in *Petits Propos Culinaires*, 30 and 34, London, 1988, 1990
Boulestin, X M, and Hill, J: *Herbs, Salads and Seasonings*, London, 1930
Bremness, L: *The Complete Book of Herbs*, London, 1988
Cost, B: *Asian Ingredients*, London, 1990
David, E: *Spices, Salt and Aromatics in the English Kitchen*, London, 1970
David, E: *Summer Cooking*, London, 1955
Evelyn, J: *Acetaria*, London, 1699
Gerard, J: *The Herball*, London, 1633 edition
Goldstein, D: *The Georgian Feast*, New York, 1993
Gordon, L: *A Country Herbal*, Exeter, 1980

Grieve, M: *Culinary Herbs and Condiments*, New York, 1971
Grieve, M: *A Modern Herbal*, London, 1931
Halici: Nevin Halici's *Turkish Cookbook*, London, 1989
Hutson, L: *The Herb Garden Cookbook*, Houston, 1992
Kalças, E: *Food from the Fields*, Izmir, 1984
Kennedy, D: *The Cuisines of Mexico*, New York, 1972
Kitchiner, W: *The Cook's Oracle*, London, 1817
Landry, R: *Les Soleils de la Cuisine*, Paris, 1967
Leyel, C F: *Salads*, London, no date
Leyel, C F: *Summer Drinks and Winter Cordials*, London, 1925
Loewenfeld, C, and Back, P: *The Complete Book of Herbs and Spices*, Newton Abbot, 1974

Olney, R: *Simple French Food*, London, 1981
Ortiz, E: *The Best of Caribbean Cooking*, London, 1975
Parkinson, J: *Paradisi in Sole*, London, 1656 edition
Parkinson, J: *Theatrum Botanicum*, London, 1640
Pruthi, J S: *Spices and Condiments*, New Delhi, 1976
Raper, E: *The Receipt Book*, London, 1924
Rodale's *Illustrated Encyclopedia of Herbs*, Emmaus, 1987
Roden, C: *A New Book of Middle Eastern Food*, London, 1985
Rohde, E S: *Culinary and Salad Herbs*, London, 1940
Rohde, E S: *A Garden of Herbs*, London, 1926
Rohde, E S: *Herbs and Herb Gardening*, London, 1936

Rundell, E: *A New System of Domestic Cookery*, London, 1843 edition
Shaida, M: *The Legendary Cuisine of Persia*, Henley, 1992
Smires, L B: *La Cuisine Marocaine*, Paris, 1971
Sotti, M L, and Beffa, M T: *Le Piante Aromatiche*, Milan, 1989
Stobart, T: *Herbs, Spices and Flavourings*, London, 1970
Teubner, C: *Kräuter und Knoblauch*, Fussen, 1993
Tsuji, S: *Japanese Cooking*, Tokyo, 1980
Uyldert, M: *De Taal der Kruiden*, Naarden, 1971
Verral, W: *A Complete System of Cookery*, London, 1759
Vilmorin-Andrieux: *Les Plantes Potagères*, Paris, 1925
White, F: *Flowers as Food*, London, 1934

ACKNOWLEDGMENTS

Author's Acknowledgments
Ted Riddell at Cheshire Herbs, Cy Hyde at Well-Sweep Herb Farm, Anthony Lyman-Dixon at Arne Herbs provided plants and helpful information on many herbs. The staff at Il giardino officinale di Casola Valsenio gave their time to show me the garden and explain their research. Bart Spices and Darégal Herbs provided herbs in oil and frozen herbs respectively.
The Lancellotti family, particularly Angelo, have been very generous with advice, ideas and recipes. Gene Bourg gave advice on Acadian and Creole cooking, Richard Hosking sent information on herbs in Japan. Paul Breman checked the text and proofs, Sasha and Elinor Breman tested recipes.
Fay Franklin and Pamela Brown at Dorling Kindersley have been patient, painstaking and helpful in their editing and Julia Worth has been imaginative and accommodating in her design for the book.

Dorling Kindersley would like to thank Ian O'Leary for his photographs; Emma Brogi for photographic assistance; Sarah Ponder for the artworks; home economists Nicola Fowler, Sunil Vijayakar and Oona van den Berg; Laura Jackson, Clare Marshall, Anna Hagenbuch and Jennie Dooge for design assistance; Jasmine Challis for nutritional information; Sarah Ereira for the index; Suzy Dittmar, Bridget Roseberry and Paul Wood for DTP work. With thanks to the following companies and individuals for their assistance: Arne Herbs, Chelsea Physic Garden, Cheshire Herbs, Rosemary Titterington at Iden Croft Herbs, Poyntzfield Herb Nursery, Suffolk Herbs, The Savill Garden, Culpeper Ltd, Fox's Spices and Geneviève Lethu, London (for tableware, pages 63–64).

Picture credits All photography by Ian O'Leary except for: Martin Norris, page 40, top.